KEEP THE FIRE BURNING

ENDORSEMENTS

It is rare to find someone who has cultivated a personal revival culture over a lifetime. It is even rarer to find someone who has been successful at empowering others to live a revival lifestyle over a lifetime. Steve and Sally Wilson have done just that! I know them personally, and they are true world changers. I would encourage you to not only buy *Keep the Fire Burning*, but to do it! I am confident that their impartations will propel you into your supernatural destiny as a world changer!

Kevin Dedmon, Pastoral staff at Bethel Church, Redding, CA

Author of *The Ultimate Treasure Hunt, Unlocking Heaven, The Risk Factor* and *Firestarters*

This book comes from hearts that faithfully said, *Keep the Fire Burning!* Steve and Sally not only say it but they have continued to cultivate faithfulness so that the fire continues to burn. I have walked with Steve and Sally in the nations of the world and have been touched by their hunger for The Kingdom of God to be manifested in the earth! They have lived out the truths in this book and they have become the very foundation, structure, faith, and power that is enabling them to see the passion which Jesus has placed in their heart come to fruition!

Read this book many times and the truths within will not be remembered in your intellect, but will become Jesus, The Truth, living and manifesting through your spirit, soul, and body! The Lamb is worthy, so *Keep the Fire Burning!*

Dr. Sam Matthews, Family of Faith Church

ICLC Apostolic Network

Keep the Fire Burning is a seeker's handbook for personal and corporate revival. With sound Biblical doctrine and inspiring testimonies, the Wilsons have crafted a roadmap that will guide the reader from ideology to an experiential destination. This book is a must read for anyone longing for supernatural expression in their life and ministry.

Carter and Diana Wood, Senior Leaders, Vertical Call

Upon first meeting Steve and Sally, it was as if we had known them for all our lives. We quickly found that even though they have much influence in the body of Christ, it is their joy to empower others. Their apostolic authority is understated in their words, but is overwhelmingly demonstrated in Godly character and power. This caliber of lifestyle validates *Keep the Fire Burning* even more than the profound truths you will read herein. Practical and vital elements of revival are clearly written about... and all the while, 'salted' with inspiring testimonies to create faith for the same miracle to happen again. Living in revival is the new norm... Steve and Sally's lives and testimonies prove it. *Keep the Fire Burning* creates a solid foundation and launching pad for everyone aspiring to initiate and host revival. On earth as it is (here) in Heaven!

Mark and Debbie Hendrickson, Dwelling Place Ministries
Author of *Supernatural Provision*

Steve and Sally Wilson invite the reader to partake from 40 years of tangible experiences with God. They marry their unwavering theology with the power of God to prophetically unveil the direction of the body of Christ for this current move of God. In all my years as a believer and the past five as an itinerant minister, I have never found a book so inspiring yet practical on empowering the body to live a supernatural lifestyle. You will receive an impartation of faith and expectancy to see God touch your church, your city and your nation.

Ahab Alhindi, Bethel Activation Ministries
Bethel Church, Redding, CA

For years I have been in search for an answer to revival. Having traveled to more than 32 countries and counting, I meet many who are in search of that same answer. Now I have it. Steve and Sally Wilson's insights and knowledge on the subject is not just textbook talk but proven Biblical concepts that will take anyone who desires into the realm of revival that only few have ever seen. That being said, I wholeheartedly endorse this work for anyone who desires to go deeper into the realm of a true revival culture.

Dr. Bennett C. Smith, Senior Pastor/Bishop,
Destiny International Fellowship of Ministries,
Destiny Center Church, Mobile, AL

Steve and Sally Wilson's pursuit of a revival lifestyle springs off the pages of *Keep the Fire Burning*, inspiring conviction and courage for others to do the same. The Wilsons' journey, with all of its victories and challenges, details a unique map of their quest for breakthrough, while providing a blueprint of living truths for those who are hungry and thirsty for more. This work is more than theory; these are dynamic truths made

ENDORSEMENTS

alive by lives yielded to the work of the Holy Spirit.

The Wilsons have not only raised up an amazing church that is changing their city and region, they carry a contagious revival presence wherever they go. Personally, I have been greatly impacted by the fruit of what they have stepped into, and I'm thrilled that this lifestyle has been captured in written form for others to receive. As a father and a mother in the faith, they are imparting a supernatural lifestyle to a generation through everything they do. Their lives are truly impacting the nations, and *Keep the Fire Burning* powerfully captures that reality.

Andy and Jami Rudd, Senior Pastors
Ardmore Harvest Fellowship

My wife and I have joyfully known Steve and Sally Wilson as friends, mentors and co-laborers for the past 13 years. Steve and his wife Sally are leaders in the Body of Christ who have earnestly pursued God and His kingdom as their foremost priority in life. They are people of integrity and honor, imparting to others their incredible wisdom and insight. We have personally been on the receiving end of their gift.

The message of revival culture is particularly pertinent at a time when revival fires are beginning to burn all over the world. Steve's message is sure to keep us from repeating the mistakes of past revivals and to *Keep the Fires Burning* for future generations.

Earl and Sylvia Ackley, Senior Pastors, Springs of Life
Eldorado Springs, MO

ENDORSEMENTS

A new era, a new move of God with a new government is at the door. The principles presented in *Keep the Fire Burning* by Steve and Sally Wilson are strategic for this time; a NOW time when we must make room for and embrace the changes coming by The Spirit of God, a Kairos time when we will be given unprecedented opportunities to move forward to fulfill the purposes for which we were created. This is not church as usual. We have not gone this way before, but God gives us apostolic leaders to pioneer and point the way forward. I have visited few churches that have cultivated a "Hot House" environment open enough to experience an awakening, and structured enough to sustain it. Dayspring is one of those. Steve and Sally are anointed apostolic gardeners planting and watering for revival. The seed is being scattered for the harvest!

Dr. Kim Maas, KIM MAAS MINISTRIES, Inc

Moorpark, CA

KEEP THE FIRE BURNING

Creating and Sustaining a Revival Culture in the Local Church

STEVE AND SALLY WILSON

1451 Clark Street, Mechanicsburg, PA 17055

globalawakening

Apostolic Network of Global Awakening
1451 Clark Street
Mechanicsburg, PA 17055

For more information on how to order this book or any of the other materials that Global Awakening offers, please contact the Global Awakening Bookstore.

Unless otherwise indicated, all scripture taken from the NEW AMERICAN STANDARD BIBLE®, Copyright ©1960, 1962, 1963, 1968, 1971, 1972, 1973, 1975, 1977, 1995 by The Lockman Foundation. Used by permission. (www.Lockman.org)

Scripture quotations are taken from the Holy Bible, New Living Translation (NLT), copyright ©1996, 2004, 2007 by Tyndale House Foundation. Used by permission of Tyndale House Publishers, Inc., Carol Stream, Illinois 60188. All rights reserved.

ISBN: 978-1-937467-74-6

Dedication

Sally and I dedicate this

to our daughter Rachel

and to our son Philip

who have lived this journey with us.

TABLE OF CONTENTS

ACKNOWLEDGEMENTS

We thank the Dayspring Family
for your faithfulness in fanning the flame of revival,
for the love and support you so faithfully show us
and for the compassion you extend to the world.

Special thanks to Farley Lewis
for his valuable suggestions and
hours of proof-reading and editing.

keep the fire burning

FOREWORD

Steve and Sally Wilson's book, *Keep the Fire Burning: Creating and Sustaining a Revival Culture in the Local Church*, is a goldmine of wisdom and information. Their book draws upon Scripture and Church history, as well as the teachings and examples of key revival leaders today. I believe this is one of the most thorough books on revival in print today, a blueprint for birthing and sustaining revival. *Keep the Fire Burning* focuses on the ingredients that come together to create the atmosphere that is needed for a revival to be sustained.

The ingredients that the Wilsons discuss include: the importance of valuing a life of power that is not religious or spooky but is "naturally supernatural;" the importance of testimonies; a theology of God's goodness, with more focus on his love than on his wrath; the importance of helping people through preaching and teaching to understand their identity in Christ in order to understand the gift of righteousness; the importance of hope and its relationship to faith and how hope creates expectancy; the importance of love; developing a culture of honor, which is consistent with heaven's value system; the importance of learning how to navigate the sometimes dangerous waters between order and life and the realization that God's order is not the same as our order; the importance of prioritizing for freedom to follow the Spirit; the importance of unity; the importance of forgiveness; and the importance of joy. Joy is what Steve and Sally call the atmosphere of the Kingdom, and this was one of the most impacting chapters for me, convicting me of not valuing the atmosphere of joy enough.

In just twelve chapters, Steve and Sally lay out a blueprint for sustaining revival. Since twelve is the number of government and the number of the disciples, it is as if each chapter is a witness, a voice, and a sent message to the church. Beginning with the belief that it is possible to create a culture of revival, and the belief that revivals are not meant to be seasonal, the Wilsons help us to see that the sovereignty of God is not the reason for the shortness of revivals. They explain that revivals often are seasonal due to various earthly, not Godly, reasons. Steve and Sally build on this foundation and explore what needs to be valued to sustain revival beyond the usual three to four years of past American revivals.

What I enjoy most about *Keep the Fire Burning* is the wisdom and clarity the book brings to the subject of revival. I appreciate the effort to ground the principles in valuing the word and the Spirit, providing a solid biblical basis for each chapter. The stories from the Wilson's lives and from Church history, as well as contemporary history, help to illustrate his biblical principles and make it easy to understand how to walk out the principles in our lives.

I have known Steve and Sally for several years and have ministered with them in several nations. I know them to be people of integrity who have a genuine hunger for revival, having experienced seasons of revival in their past. I agree with them that we are presently in the beginning of a visitation of God around the world that should be welcomed and highly valued. When Steve first approached me about the subject of this book, I told him I thought it was a great idea and would be most beneficial to the Church. I am glad he committed to this labor of love and finished *Keep the Fire Burning*. I am glad to promote the book, its subject, and Steve and Sally Wilson. I am excited to welcome *Keep the Fire Burning* to the books written in earlier days, as a welcome addition and very applicable for our times.

Dr. Randy Clark
Founder and President of Global Awakening
Mechanicsburg, PA
Author of "There is More" and "Essential Guide to Healing"

keep the fire burning

INTRODUCTION

Sally and I have had the privilege of participating in the birth of revival on three continents: first in Africa where we served as missionaries, then in England, and finally back here in the United States. In each of these diverse situations, we learned valuable lessons, which God has used to create a deep hunger for a sustained move of the Holy Spirit.

For the last 30 years we have given ourselves to the task of learning to foster a culture of revival in every aspect of church life. We have sought to create an environment where the presence of God is central, where people find their identity, where a culture of honor sustains relationships, and where each member of the body is compelled by love to reach out at every opportunity to manifest the goodness of God.

This book comes out of the things we have learned in seeking to establish this kind of culture. We have tried to be honest about some of the mistakes we have made, as well as, some of the victories we have experienced. In no way do we come as experts, but we want to share what we have learned, so that together we can nurture revival and stir up an awakening.

Before writing this, we sat with some of our leadership and together we worked on compiling a list of the things that have helped us the most, both in our teaching and in practice. This list of things served as keys in transitioning our local body from simply believing for revival to being a church that has begun to live in a sustained revival culture. Each of these topics has become a chapter, which fit together to create a revival culture. We have found that each has played a significant part in releasing more of the presence of God among us.

We have chosen not to deal with the obvious – prayer. Prayer was, is, and always will be the fountainhead for revival. Every book on revival tells this story; there has never been a revival in history that has not been birthed in powerful, believing prayer. If prayer does not have a primary place in the church, the other topics we are presenting will be meaningless adjustments. Prayer has been and is foundational for ushering in revival and in developing a revival culture. Dayspring was birthed in prayer and will be sustained by prayer. We have had seasons in which prayer flowed with a passion and others in which it was hard work. But, never the less, the fire of prayer and intercession must be kept burning.

Daniel Nash was a great example of this. Although he is almost unknown in church history, he was the secret weapon during the Second Great Awakening. Nash was the primary intercessor for Finney. Not only did he pray during the meetings, but he went to the cities where Finney planned to go and opened the heavens so breakthrough would come when Finney began his meetings in the city. Nash's intercession was of such significance in Finney's breakthroughs that a few weeks after Nash's death, Finney stopped his meetings and began a bible school.

We also have not included a chapter on hosting the presence of God - not because this is not important. We had intended it to be the first chapter, but as we wrote we realized that hosting the presence of God was woven into each chapter. It is a core foundation for all aspects of revival.

REVIVAL OR AWAKENING

The words revival and awakening are sometimes used interchangeably. For the sake of clarity in this book we want to explain our usage.

We tend to use the word revival to describe an outpouring of the Spirit in a church or locality to such a degree that the church becomes passionate about the Lord. In this atmosphere Christians are revived and sinners are saved. We think of revival primarily as an inward focus at the beginning, then as Christians are stirred, they begin reaching out to those in their circle of influence and the lost start to come in.

We see awakening as broader in meaning. In an awakening not only do Christians become awakened or conscious of the demands of the gospel on their lives but also whole communities are affected. The focus of this book is on building a revival culture in the local church in the belief that as the life of the Spirit flows out from the church the revival will become an awakening.

As far as we have found the word awakening was first used by Jonathan Edwards in connection with revival to describe what was happening in Northampton in 1735. In the year following the breakout of revival in the church he pastored, nearly the whole town was converted. The revival then spread rapidly through New England and the North East to become what we call the First Great Awakening. Edwards wrote about an awakening of conscience among the people.[1]

This distinction was typified in Brazil last year. Great revival meetings were taking place and across the street prostitutes were soliciting customers. When the pastor was asked how this could be, he said, "We have revival, but what we need is awakening." An awakening is accompanied by societal transformation. Both the First Great Awakening under Jonathan Edwards and the Second Great Awakening with Charles Finney profoundly transformed American culture. We believe that Church history will look back at the outpouring in Toronto and recognize it as an awakening, not necessarily because of the effects on Canada but because of the millions of salvations and the societal transformations that have resulted from those touched by the revival.

In the British Great Awakening under the leadership of the Wesley brothers and George Whitefield, the societal change was profound. One archbishop wrote, "Wesley practically changed the outlook and even the character of the English nation."[2] During the course of this awakening there were over 1.25 million conversions; this meant that almost 25% of the population of England turned to Christ. Some historians have credited this massive move toward genuine Christianity with keeping Britain from plunging into the kind of revolution that took place in France.[3]

We would add one final characteristic to our definition of awakening. During the awakening in Britain, Wesley activated the people for the work of the ministry. In fact it was the use of lay preachers that caused him the most trouble with the religious establishment. We believe this was a precursor to the awakening that is being birthed in the earth today. As the awakening grows, more and more of the body of Christ is being equipped and activated to do the work of the ministry.

Finally, a revival culture creates in every member of the body, a hunger to live a naturally supernatural lifestyle, living their lives as carriers of His presence.

CHAPTER ONE

Creating a Revival Culture

They put new wine into fresh wineskins, and both are preserved.

Matthew 9:17

Our journey into a revival culture began in northern Kenya where Sally and I along with our children, Rachel and Philip were serving as missionaries. We had the call of God on our lives and had given ourselves to serve Him. Although we had experienced the leading of the Spirit as we moved into ministry, we were not open to the baptism or gifts of the Holy Spirit. While in college I had an experience with the Holy Spirit but had rejected it when I allowed myself to get offended at a charismatic meeting. An immature leader foolishly implied that salvation was not miraculous. In reaction, I adopted a cessationist view and in fact one of the confessions I made to Sally before we married was that "I used to speak in tongues." So we chose to serve with a very conservative mission board.

While we were on our first furlough, Sally was baptized in the Spirit at a women's prayer meeting. After three years on the mission field, I recognized the need for more and had mellowed my anti-charismatic stance but was not ready to face the consequences of stepping back into things of the Spirit. So, I was happy for her and secretly envious of her new relationship with God.

Almost as soon as we returned to Kenya I was confronted with my own powerlessness. One afternoon the nurse on our station sent for me to help her with a patient. When I got to the dispensary there was a girl perhaps ten years of age on the examination table. The nurse told me that she could find nothing medically wrong with her but that she was dying. As I looked at the girl I saw my first demon. Clearly, the problem was not medical but demonic and I had no answers. I knew I should have had the authority to deal with this but did not!

I walked away heart sick and the little girl died. As soon as I got to the house I fell on my face and surrendered to what I knew to be true. I needed an encounter with the Holy Spirit. I made a commitment to God that "never again would I stand in the face of the enemy without the power of the Spirit." The Holy Spirit gently reminded me that I had been touched by the power of God but I had not stewarded it. He asked me if I was willing to pay the price and I made a commitment to never again quench His presence. His grace covered my weakness and in a moment my life was forever changed.

God moved quickly on our behalf and had us seconded by our mission board to a windmill project. This move took us out from under the strict anti-charismatic rules of the mission and landed us as pastors of an Anglican church in Thika, Kenya. Almost immediately a significant move of God broke out. A small prayer meeting in our home quickly grew until the place was overflowing with people desperate for the presence of God. Miracles, salvations, and midnight baptisms became common as we found ourselves riding a wave of the Spirit. It was our first taste of revival and it ruined us for anything less.

Unfortunately, the Mission we were with was not as excited as we were. They called us in and asked us to sign a statement that we would never again speak in tongues in public. When we would not do it, they gave us the right boot of fellowship by revoking our work permit. This forced us to leave the country.

ENGLAND

After leaving Kenya we moved to England to work with leaders we had met while in Kenya and to be part of an incredible movement of the Spirit. The Holy Spirit had visited the nation through the charismatic movement and when the religious establishment rejected the Spirit, hundreds of new churches were birthed. The Restoration movement was a gathering of leaders from many of those groupings that had begun to work together for the purpose of seeing the whole nation touched for Jesus. Powerful conferences drew thousands to worship and the air was electric with possibility. But as so often happens, relationships did not stand the test of success and division began to dismantle what God had built. Personal agendas caused the breakup of the team and resulted in a drift toward individualism. We once again tasted revival and even the potential of an awakening, only to see it slip away. But we saw the need for a greater understanding of honor if a move of God was to be sustained.

Despite the difficulties, we were profoundly touched and changed during our years in England. We were able to shed cumbersome religious baggage as we experienced freedom in the Spirit. We found life-changing relationships that have shaped who we are in ministry. We began to understand the importance of the five-fold ministry gifts to the body, not as a hierarchal structure but as aspects of the fullness of Christ that are needed for the Body to be fully equipped and released in ministry.

While in England we embraced healing as a vital component in the gospel. John Wimber visited several times and brought a fresh theology for healing. We also had the privilege of interacting with Ian Andrews. Ian has a powerful healing ministry and operates with great accuracy in the word of knowledge. Through time ministering alongside him we received an impartation and began to see some significant healings ourselves. We even began to learn to take it to the streets.

One weekend we were hosting a leaders' retreat and Ian had a dream, which has affected the way we view revival. At that time healing happened largely from the platform, the model used most by healing evangelists. In his dream Ian saw a "mountain of men" and the Lord spoke to him that there would come a day when healing was no longer going to be a platform exercise, but that the whole body of Christ was going to be equipped to participate in the ministry of healing the sick. This experience profoundly shaped our understanding of the nature of revival culture. We see revival culture as an atmosphere where every believer is equipped to live a naturally supernatural lifestyle.

REVIVAL IS COMING

As our expectation grew for what we knew God could do, we found ourselves deeply hungry for more. God had birthed in us an insatiable thirst for a move of God that would sweep the whole earth. In 1990, Sally and I along with our two children were living in Leeds. Three years before, we had planted a church in an urban area called Chapletown and, although it had grown well, we were feeling unsettled. As we sought God about the future of the work, we heard clearly that we were to move back to the U.S. to be in position "for the revival that is coming that will touch the whole earth."

In obedience, we packed up our family and moved back to the States in mid-1991. After a couple of years working with a church plant in Atlanta, Georgia, and then a stint at ORU working on our Master's degrees, the Lord directed us to Springfield, Missouri. If He had given us a choice, we would not have chosen Springfield. We had developed a strong distaste for anything religious and, if the religious spirit had a navel, Springfield was it. We have since repented and have come to love our city, but it took several years of attitude adjustments. We began to see our city the way God does: full of hope. The living hope He gives us has proved to be another key to sustaining revival.

We came to Springfield because a group asked us to help a struggling church. As soon as we arrived, the church began experiencing waves of renewal. The revival fires burning in Toronto began to touch us, but not everyone liked it. The Holy Spirit seemed to be stirring up the proverbial hornet's nest. Some people wanted more order and were nervous with what they saw as chaos. Others were excited about what God was doing, even if it got a little messy at times. The church ended up choosing order over life, and we were voted out. But God was giving us another key to a revival culture: learning to walk the tension between order and life.

We wanted to shake the dust of Springfield off our feet, leave and never look back. But the Lord sovereignly directed us to plant a church focused on revival on the opposite side of town. Even though we were reluctant, the Wednesday after we were voted out, with almost a foot of snow on the ground, some 35 hungry souls showed up at our house. So began Dayspring. The first few years we focused on building a core of committed people and renovating an abandoned church property.

Over the next few years we experienced several waves of renewal. Most of our leadership went to Brownsville and many were profoundly touched by what God was doing there. It even briefly touched our city, but the religious establishment made sure it didn't go too far. We had Rodney Howard Brown pay us a visit and he released joy into us as a people, which has become another foundation of our revival culture. As we reflect back on those years, we realize that even though we did not see fully what we were expecting, each wave of renewal increased the level of the presence of God in our midst.

REVIVAL IS HERE!

Fast-forward to 2009 - Dutch Sheets was invited to come to Dayspring for a series of meetings organized by the Missouri Prayer Network. In the closing service Dutch gave a prophetic word over Dayspring that drew a line in the sand. He made a declaration that from that night we were to change the vocabulary we used regarding revival. We were no longer to say that revival is coming but were to begin to declare that revival is here. We were to change from speaking about the move of God in the future tense to speaking of it in the present tense. The shout that rose up was amazing as many grabbed hold of the word. But the word didn't end there. Dutch went on to say that revival had not come as we expected. But that it had come as an infant that needed to be nurtured.

Now, I love revivals and love reading the accounts of moves of God whenever I can get my hands on them. I have dreamed of revival and taught on revival but never in my wildest imagination had I thought about an infant revival. Immediately, my mind went into overdrive with more questions than answers. Images of bottles and dirty diapers flooded my head as I grappled with words that I knew in my heart came from God. What does an infant revival look like? How do you take care of it? What do you feed it to make it grow? How do you measure the growth?

The primary thrust of the word Dutch give us was that we needed to create a culture of revival in the church so that the revival fire could grow. As soon as the word was given we began to ask God how to do what He was asking us to do. The challenge we faced was that we only knew how to do what we knew how to do. Many of the values we held had helped create the atmosphere of God's presence that we enjoyed. We did not want to lose those, but we knew that to become whom He was calling us to be would require more than we had.

SUSTAINING REVIVAL

Why do we need a revival culture? Experience and church history teach us that when the Holy Spirit is poured out, new life is breathed into the church. But over a period of time the excitement of the move of God gets displaced as weaknesses in the structure of the local church or organization are exposed. If the culture of the church has not been prepared to deal with this correctly, the move of God falters on the fragility of human emotion. Countless examples can be given of genuine movements of the Spirit that ended in discord, division, personal moral failure, or the burnout of a key figure.

Because of this cyclical pattern of revival, some have asked if revival is intended to sustain or if it is the plan of God to visit His people to strengthen them only for brief periods in history. This appears logical since in all of nature things tend to degenerate. From the time sin entered the world through the human race there has been a law at work that causes everything to fall apart, decay, and to die. Apart from the intervention of God, things don't get better naturally; they naturally get worse. Revival is God's way of halting and reversing the spiritual and moral decline of His church to bring it back to His intention. But after multiple moves of God having ended prematurely because of relational upheaval, is it realistic to expect a sustained move of God? Can revival be sustained so that it grows to the point where it can affect the whole earth?

The second law of thermodynamics in simple terms teaches that in the physical realm things tend to run down.[1] A spring-driven watch will run until all the energy in the spring has been used; it will then stop until more energy is put into the spring. One word used to describe process is entropy, defined as a measure of disorder. So, not only do things tend to run down, but they also tend to move from order to disorder.

While this scenario appears to describe our experience with revival quite accurately, it does not describe God's intention. The word of God gives sufficient evidence to show that it is His intention that His presence dwells continually with and in His people. A cursory read through the Book of Acts shows that the early church lived in a state of revival for years; so the idea of sustained revival should not be that surprising. The same law in thermodynamics when applied to biology states that it is the flow of energy that maintains both order and life.[2] Therefore, if we can learn to live with a continual injection of His Divine energy, then things can run up instead of run down. If this is true, then living with a constant awareness of His presence and power become the primary key to sustaining a move of His Spirit.

KEEP THE FIRE BURNING

Charles Finney was a leader in the choir when he was converted and soon after became a key figure in the Second Great Awakening. He witnessed revival almost everywhere he traveled, leading him to believe that revival was the norm for church. Although he was raised Presbyterian, as he began to experience revival, he moved away from his strict Calvinist roots that viewed revival as strictly a sovereign act and began to teach that there was human responsibility in laying the groundwork for a move of God. In fact he wrote, "Revival is no more a miracle than a crop of wheat."[3]

He believed that, if the conditions were met, revival was the expected outcome. A farmer, who prepares the ground and plants the seeds, expects a harvest. Finney believed that if the conditions and atmosphere were created for revival, then it was a foregone conclusion that revival would come. It is in this same vein that we see the need to develop a revival culture in the church that prepares the way for God's sovereign activity and creates an atmosphere in which the move of God can thrive and sustain.

As co-laborers with God, we prepare the altar and God sends the fire. Even after the fire falls, it was the role of the Old Testament priests to steward the fire, so that it would never die. As priests of the New Covenant we are called to prepare a place where God will come and dwell, a place where He fully releases His activity among us. We are called to develop a revival culture in the church, which prepares the way for God's sovereign activity and creates an atmosphere in which the move of God can thrive and sustain.

REVIVAL CULTURE

When we speak of a revival culture, what are we referring to? Culture can be defined as a set of beliefs and values that govern actions. So when we refer to a revival culture we are referring to a set of spiritual beliefs and values that create an atmosphere conducive to revival. These beliefs and values create an environment where the activity of the Holy Spirit is normal, and the highest value is placed on making room for the presence of God. The life of intimacy this produces is expressed in worship but extends beyond meetings, making it possible for every believer to live with a constant awareness of the presence of God.

It is also a culture that celebrates our identity in Christ as sons and daughters with access to the resources of heaven. A revival culture fosters an atmosphere of unconditional love and honor within the body, helping each believer maintain right and healthy relationships. The identity found in a revival culture changes church because it changes the motivation behind the actions. In a revival culture members of the church still serve and give, but they do it all from a place of acceptance and value and not to receive acceptance and value.

Finally, revival culture is not passive; it is living and active which means it must flow out of the building and onto the streets. The personal encounters that people have with the presence of God should cause the life of the Spirit to naturally flow out through them to those around them. This means that a church creating a revival culture must have a deliberate strategy for equipping and activating the whole body to do the work of the ministry. For most of us this is going to require a new paradigm for church life.

A NEW WINESKIN

Even though we don't like to admit it, we all have set ways of doing things. We may speak against someone else's liturgy, but we all have a liturgy we revert to… yes, even Charismatics and Pentecostals. Our liturgy just doesn't feel like a liturgy because it is ours. To get a different result we must do something different. Creating a revival culture requires giving freedom for the Holy Spirit to move in every aspect of our services, as well as our lives. For most of us this is a challenge because we like things the way we like things.

When Jesus called Matthew to be His disciple, the religious leaders were incensed that He would associate Himself with those perceived to be sinners. Jesus' response was to challenge the religious framework that held them captive. *Nor do men put new wine in old wineskins; otherwise the wineskins burst, and the wine pours out, and the wineskins are ruined; but they put new wine into fresh wineskins, and both are preserved* (Matt. 9:17). To embrace the new things that God wants to do in His church requires that we abandon inflexible structures and embrace freedom in the Holy Spirit.

When the Holy Spirit is poured out, the vessel into which He is poured must be flexible enough to contain what God wants to do. If not, the structure will break and both the wine and the skin will be destroyed. This accurately describes some of the devastation that has tragically ended several moves of God in revival history. New wine must go into a new structure because it requires flexibility. Notice the concern over the wineskin; both old and new need to be preserved. The context is a move from the old to a new working of His grace. The application is that revival touching our church will not sustain unless the structure is flexible enough to change and make room for the work of the Holy Spirit. The structure doesn't create the revival, but it provides an atmosphere where it can grow unhindered and at the same time be protected. If the structure is sufficiently flexible, the wine of the Spirit can move and grow indefinitely, allowing revival to be sustained and awakening to affect the entire community.

CROSS POLLINATION

Perhaps the most directional word we received during the season following Dutch's word was about the rivers that watered the Garden of Eden. God spoke that "Just as four rivers watered the Garden of Eden (Gen. 2:10-14), we needed to be watered by four different streams each year." We had been relatively self-sufficient as a church. But, as we meditated on what we had heard, we realized we were in danger of becoming ingrown, believing that all we needed was in the house. The truth is that God has designed us to need one another and He reminded us that, the streams make glad the city of God (Ps. 46:4).

In response we began to invite some diverse ministries to make a spiritual deposit into Dayspring. Dutch Sheets had already touched us with his word on the need to grow a revival culture. Bob Hartley came and deposited hope and a victorious eschatology. We linked up with Randy Clark and the Global Awakening team who have profoundly impacted us in the area of healing and miracles. Bill Johnson was with us as part of the healing schools and impacted us deeply with his teaching on hosting the presence. We also invited Kevin Dedmon from Bethel and he deposited a hunger to live a naturally supernatural lifestyle.

CHAPTER TWO

Life of Power: Naturally Supernatural

*…Signs and wonders and by various miracles and by
gifts of the Holy Spirit…*

Hebrews 2:4

I remember one particularly powerful night in Northern Kenya. We had been installing a water system in a Turkana village when the witch doctor, named Nyangodia, began to ask questions about why we were doing this for them. It led to an opportunity for the gospel to be shared and, after several hours of going through the plan of salvation, he made a radical commitment to follow Christ. By this time it was three in the morning, but he assembled the whole village and proceeded to tell them everything we had shared with him. By daybreak the whole village had made a commitment to follow Jesus. We were completely undone!

We left early the next day and learned later that, just after we left, someone came to the village and asked Nyangodia to come help a woman who had been bitten by a snake. His testimony was that before he thought about it, he grabbed the little bag of rocks and bones that he used as a witch doctor and went to the village to heal her. He told us that, when he got there and saw the sick woman, he remembered what he had done the night before. He began to ask himself the question, "If I now serve this Jesus, He must be more powerful than this (referring to his little bag of charms), otherwise, there would have been no reason to believe in Him?" So, he prayed a simple prayer, "Jesus, You must be more powerful than the spirits I have known; You must have the power to heal this woman. I don't know how; so You do it!" Instantly the woman was healed.

SUPERNATURAL WORLDVIEW

Tribal culture in Kenya has a spiritual worldview. People understood and believed in the supernatural and considered it just as real as the natural realm. The dark side of this belief structure gave room for witch doctors to wield demonic power that held people in bondage, mostly through fear. However, when confronted with the power of the gospel, they were open and expectant, believing that the God who saved them could and would also move in miraculous power on their behalf.

In the West we don't think this way and, as a result, miss many opportunities for God to break into the natural realm with His power and glory. Our primarily naturalistic worldview makes it challenging to accept that the unseen realm is just as real as the natural world around us. For many Christians, our expectations of what God can and will do come from our experience, rather than from the truth of Scripture.

Our cultural understanding has been allowed to shape our beliefs and to explain our experience. We then interpret the Bible through the lenses of our experience, which eventually becomes our doctrine. So, instead of pursuing the miracles, we have effectively made religious excuses for why we don't experience them. We justify our powerlessness because it is easier than facing it.

This means that to sustain revival our churches must make a cultural shift to a more spiritually expectant worldview. To achieve this, a revival culture creates an environment where the works of God are regularly in front of the people so that the supernatural realm becomes just as real as the natural. This change of perspective then opens the body to the possibility of Divine intervention in every area of life.

In fact it is God's intention that every Christian live a naturally super-natural lifestyle, with the gifts of the Spirit in regular operation. Today we have the privilege of living in a time of extraordinary outpouring of the power and presence of God, making access to the power of the Spirit as natural as breathing.

I remember when we returned to the village and heard Nyangodia's testimony. Even though I had been raised in Africa I grew up with a fairly skeptical western worldview. As I heard his story, I felt a deep conviction of the Spirit that my expectation of God's ability had too many lim-its. I repented for the powerless view of the Gospel I had believed and preached, and I asked the Holy Spirit to help me break out of my natural thinking so that the realm of the Spirit would become just as real. From that moment the miracles began to increase through my life.

GOSPEL OF POWER

A primary component in the harvest is a return to the Gospel of pow-er that Jesus lived. We will never get His results until we are committed to using His methods. Demonstrations of power were central to His mes-sage of the Kingdom of God. These miracles validated His message (Acts 2:22), but they were more than that. The miracles were an expression of the message.

When we look at the life of Paul we see the same pattern. *In the power of (attesting miracles) signs and wonders, in the power of the Spirit; so that from Jerusalem and round about as far as Illyricum I have fully preached the gospel of Christ* (Rom. 15:19). At the birth of the church miracles served as a vital part of the Gospel message. In fact Paul states here that the Gospel is only fully preached when it is accompanied by the miraculous demonstration of the power of God. If the church preaches a powerless message, she will be a powerless church.

Unfortunately, the message now being preached in most western churches bears little resemblance to the original, and consequently, we have neglected the miraculous component of the gospel. This potential to miss a crucial element of the truth is what the writer of Hebrews addresses. He warns us to pay close attention to the things that we have heard in scripture so we don't drift away and … *neglect so great a salvation?* (Heb. 2:3).

The challenge is to pay close attention so we don't drift away from the truth. It is easy to begin to let experience dictate truth, rather than the Word. If we don't see many miracles, we tend to form theologies that explain this lack. The Word says clearly that we are prone to drift away from our great salvation and that a part of that great salvation is the working of the Holy Spirit in and through us, validating the word with signs, wonders, miracles, and gifts of the Holy Spirit.

The next verse makes this connection clear, *God also testifying with them, both by signs and wonders and by various miracles and by gifts of the Holy Spirit according to His own will* (Heb. 2:4). This is absolutely stunning. In the context of not neglecting our great salvation the writer tells us that whenever our great salvation is proclaimed, it is to be validated by the miraculous.

Normal Christian life is – "God testifying with them." God didn't start us out, and then leave us to do it on our own. His dealings with mankind have been marked by the miraculous since the beginning of time. God has always intended to testify with us. He gave us the Holy Spirit who testifies to us and through us as we present the Gospel (John 15:26, 27). To see the harvest come in, the church must return to an expectation of miraculous power validating the message of salvation.

In Matthew 13:30, we are told in the parable of the wheat and tares that both the wheat and tares grow together. When they come to maturity, the wheat is gathered into the barns and the tares are gathered and burned. Notice here that both the wheat and the tares come to maturity at the same time. This means that evil is maturing at the same time as the gospel of the kingdom is advancing. When we see evil rising at an unprecedented rate, don't be distracted; the Church is maturing at the same time! The harvest is ready and the level of God's presence is rising in the earth. Focus on what God is doing and participate in His glory being revealed.

THE IMPOSSIBLE IS NORMAL

One of our friends named Chiharu noticed a very sick young man whom we will refer to as Bryan, a tenant in the same building where she lived. She eventually got the opportunity to sit and talk in a common area of the building and found out more about him. He had pain all over his body, a hole in his liver, a leaking heart, and his kidneys were failing. He had just been started on regular dialysis; the doctors had told him it was too late to save the kidneys and there was very little hope for his other organs. He was put on a waiting list for a kidney transplant, but was told that even if he had surgery, he had only a two percent chance of survival. But when God gets involved all the percentages change.

She brought him to a service, and the church gathered around him to pray for healing. When they started praying, he could barely walk, and his pain level was 9 on a scale of 1 to 10, with 10 being "take me to the hospital." As they prayed they saw a slight improvement, so they prayed several more times until the pain was almost completely gone and he was smiling.

In the car on the way home, Bryan talked excitedly about the miracle God had done for him. And by the time they arrived home, his pain had completely gone and he demonstrated that he could jump, something he had not been able to do since the onset of his illness. When Chiharu took him to his room their landlord was there to assist and witnessed the change in him. Today, two years later, he is still alive, his voice is strong and he has no pain. Our God makes the impossible normal!

SUPERNATURAL TOOLS

Don't miss the moment! Supernatural tools are available to us to do the work of the kingdom. The Holy Spirit is equipping every believer who is willing with a fresh endowment of power. Paul tells the church:

> But to each one is given the manifestation of the Spirit for the common good. 8 For to one is given the word of wisdom through the Spirit, and to another the word of knowledge according to the same Spirit; 9 to another faith by the same Spirit, and to another gifts of healing by the one Spirit, 10 and to another the effecting of miracles, and to another prophecy, and to another the distinguishing of spirits, to another various kinds of tongues, and to another the interpretation of tongues. (1 Cor. 12:7-10)

The person of the Holy Spirit has made a vast array of His gifts available to us. If we have received the baptism of the Holy Spirit, the gifts are for us. Each one is given at least one manifestation of the Spirit to be used in our interaction with others. Notice that it says that these gifts are for the common good – they are given to us for others. God's intention is that the people of God use the gifts so that those around them can have a legitimate encounter with our supernatural God.

The gifts of the Spirit are the tools that enable us to move in the supernatural realm. To live a naturally supernatural lifestyle requires that we familiarize ourselves with these tools so that we become proficient. As we practice these gifts and make them part of our lifestyle, we realize that the miraculous realm is open for any believer who is willing to take the risk to step out in faith. Particularly, as we move out in power evangelism, several of these gifts open the doors.

HEALING AND MIRACLES

In the list of gifts of the Spirit, miracles and healing are just as common as tongues or prophesy. Healing and miracles are not some super gifts that the elite attain to; they are to become normal life for the believer. To be in fellowship with God is to learn to live in a culture where miracles are normal.

When our expectation is set by our experience rather than by the truth of the Word, it will prove difficult to move into the realm of the supernatural. As Christians, we speak and act out of the things we believe. Paul quotes David when he tells the Corinthians that ... *having the same spirit of faith, according to what is written, 'I believed, therefore I spoke,' we also believe, therefore also we speak* (2 Cor. 4:13). The confidence to speak with boldness comes from what we truly believe. So, if we want to move in greater boldness we will need to strengthen our belief. We need to believe that heaven is speaking and that we can hear the voice of God and convey His heart to those around us. This applies particularly to moving out in the miraculous.

If we believe God can and will move through us, we will speak with confidence. But if there is a doubt in us, we will hesitate and miss the opportunity. This belief also extends to how confident we are that God wants to heal. If we are unsure of God's disposition toward healing, then we will hesitate to pray for someone. But if we know that God's heart is healing and He wants to do it through us, then we will press in until it becomes a reality in our lives.

We need to settle it in our hearts that healing and miracles are for today as a continuation of the ministry of Jesus[1] and as an essential part of the gospel message. They are for today because our God is a healer with healing in His nature. Every time He heals it is an evident expression of His goodness. He is Jehovah Rapha, the God who heals, mends, cures, repairs and makes thoroughly whole[2] (Exod. 15:26).

Miracles are for today because Jesus purchased them for us in the atonement, (Isa. 53:4, 5, Matt. 8:16, 17) and they flow from a life full of the Holy Spirit. We need to believe they are for today because they are normal in a kingdom culture. From the time we were children we have prayed – "on earth as it is in heaven." It is time to believe what we have prayed. And finally, we need to believe that miracles are for today because each miracle shines as a manifestation of the glory of God. Settle it! God wants to demonstrate His power today through us!

WORD OF KNOWLEDGE

A gift that works closely with healing and miracles is the "word of knowledge." When God revealed Himself as the Lord our healer, He did it through a word of knowledge (Exod. 15:22-26). The water at Marah was healed when Moses obeyed the word of knowledge to throw a certain stick into the water.

Words of knowledge are sometimes connected with healing. When God wants to heal, He often speaks the word needed to unlock our faith. The word of knowledge is like a stick thrown into bitter waters; catch the stick and get the healing. This is consistent with what we read in scripture *He sent His word and healed them, and delivered them from their destructions* (Ps. 107:20). The Word of God releases healing.

The word of knowledge carries with it the healing power of God. It comes as a fragment of information from the Spirit and is given as a key to unlock the situation. The word of knowledge does not come from any natural source; it is a piece of information that comes from the Holy Spirit and is given for a specific purpose. In our experience when a word of knowledge is given, people are often healed even before we pray. Last year we witnessed a totally deaf girl receive hearing in both ears simply by the word of knowledge given when we were in a meeting in Brazil with Randy Clark. Part of the wonder was how a deaf person was able to respond to a spoken word of knowledge!

PRACTICE THE SUPERNATURAL

The word practice sounds wrong. In our religious mindset, if it isn't perfect, we shouldn't do it. One of the greatest gifts we have received, however, is the right to get it wrong without condemnation. This allows us to try and fail in the process. When a child is learning to walk, we celebrate even one step; so it should be as we learn to walk in the supernatural realm. The revelation we get is at best partial (1 Cor. 13:12). This verse applies specifically to prophecy, another crucial gift in power evangelism. People have no idea that God still speaks today. When we release words of edification or encouragement to people, the stage is set for them to respond to God. Our faith grows as we step out and see God move.

The writer of Hebrews challenges believers to ...*consider how to stimulate one another to love and good deeds...* (Heb. 10:24). Literally, think up ways to push each other to go further. There is something powerful that happens when we look for opportunities to challenge each other to step out in the supernatural. In a group, we are more likely to take a risk and push past our natural hesitancy. All of us need the encouragement to break out of the comfortable and step into life where the supernatural becomes normal.

One of the tools we have used effectively in practicing the supernatural is "treasure hunts"[3] introduced to us by Kevin Dedmon. These exercises combine prophecy, word of knowledge, and healing in a practical way. On one recent treasure hunt, Christina, a young lady on the team, heard three words of knowledge, blue dress, American flag and back pain.

Twenty minutes later her team went to a farmer's market and seated behind a table was a woman in a blue dress. The table had an American flag-themed tablecloth and directly in front of her was a photo of another American flag. When asked, the woman confirmed that she had back pain so serious that she could not walk without assistance, and she was willing to receive prayer for it. When the team prayed and commanded the back to be healed, God showed up and honored their faith. The woman was instantly healed. She stood up unassisted and showed them her new freedom from pain by stretching, walking, and bending. She was quite surprised and very happy to be pain-free.

News of the healing got around at the farmer's market and interest in what the team was doing ran high. People began to give them gifts - woodcarvings, food items, etc. - and the whole atmosphere of the market changed. *And the name of the Lord Jesus was held in high honor* (Acts 19:17).

GATE OF HEAVEN

The first mention of God having a dwelling place among men was in the life of Jacob. It happened the night he was running from his brother, laid down in the middle of nowhere and had a dream about a ladder reaching into heaven and angels ascending and descending. *When Jacob awoke from his sleep, he thought, 'Surely the Lord is in this place, and I was not aware of it.' 17 He was afraid and said, 'How awesome is this place! This is none other than the house of God; this is the gate of heaven'* (Gen. 28:16-17).

I am always struck by Jacob's comment about being unaware of God's presence. I don't know about you, but I have been there many times in my life. Often I have realized later that God was present doing something, but I was too busy or too distracted to realize it. Just because we don't feel Him does not make His presence any less real.

Jacob's mention of the House of God is the first reference in Scripture to a dwelling place of God on the earth. This was before the tabernacle in the wilderness, before the tabernacle of David, and before the temple of Solomon.

Prophetically, it is a reference to the church and also the individuals who make up the Body of Christ. The dwelling place of God had no buildings, just a person. The power of the gospel is that through the cross we become the dwelling place of God.

Because the house of God is people who are the temple of the Holy Spirit, church can happen wherever we are. Jacob did not understand this and wanted to set up a pillar to memorialize the place, but wherever Jacob stopped that night would have been the place that God showed up.

Jacob's acknowledgement of his encounter went a step further. Remember he said the place was ...*the house of God; this is the gate of heaven.* The house of God is the gate of heaven. Bill Johnson's teaching has profoundly influenced our understanding of this passage.[4] If the church (the body of Christ) hosts the presence of the Spirit of God, then by definition there is a gate of heaven present with access to heaven's reality. When we become a dwelling place of God, we also become a gate of heaven. Heaven can reach through us to transform the lives of those around us. If people can get to us, they can get to God. As a walking gateway, we become the open heaven to our work place. We are literally a miracle waiting to happen.

Nate led a treasure hunting team in Eldorado Springs, Missouri this past fall. They came across a lady in the park who was sitting on a park bench. Their clues were park and a color, maybe green - which she had on. They approached her and told her they were on a treasure hunt and thought that she was on their list. They then proceeded to ask her if she had any of the conditions that they had written down. She ended up having almost all of the conditions on their list including lower back pain and neuropathy in the hands and feet. They prayed and after the second prayer the back pain was completely gone. When the team got back to the church to discuss what happened on the treasure hunt, one of the other teams had met the same lady just after she had been prayed for and she told them that she was completely astounded that God would heal her. As we will see in the next chapter, the testimonies of what God is doing have become like fuel on the fire of revival.

CHAPTER THREE

Testimonies: Key to Sustaining Faith

They overcame ... by the word of their testimony;

Revelation 12:11

As we began to create a revival culture in Dayspring, we almost immediately began to see an increase in the number of physical healings during our services. With each breakthrough the anticipation grew and it seemed the expectation for "more" increased every time we met. However, over a several month period we noticed a disturbing pattern. We would see several profound healings, then the frequency of healings would seem to wane, followed by several weeks where little happened. Then suddenly a significant healing would be shared and the excitement level would return, but after a few weeks it would stagnate. As much as we tried to rationalize or make what we were experiencing feel normal, we recognized we were missing something.

In praying about this cyclical pattern, the Lord began to speak to us about the place and power of testimony. He started by taking us to the book of Psalms where David tells the story of the Sons of Ephraim. They were well-equipped soldiers that faced a battle they should have won but, instead, turned and ran from the enemy. David writes, *The sons of*

Ephraim were archers equipped with bows, yet they turned back in the day of battle. They did not keep the covenant of the Lord and refused to walk in His law; they forgot His deeds and His miracles that He had shown them (Ps. 119:9-11). What went wrong?

There are two things. First, they were unfaithful in keeping the law and in fact had refused to. But look closely at the second problem. They forgot the things God had done for them; they forgot all the miracles He had performed. Grasp the implication here. They were fully equipped soldiers with everything they needed to win, but the sons of Ephraim ran from battle because they forgot the testimony. They didn't remember the wonderful things God had done; so, they lost confidence.

We realized that on some measure this was happening to us. As a discipline the Lord had me make a list of all the miracles I had seen in my life, and for over a year I kept it in the front of my Bible. I was dismayed at how much I had forgotten.

When John wrote to the churches, he listed *testimony* as one of the weapons that the people of God would use to overcome ... *because of the blood of the Lamb and because of the word of their testimony...* (Rev. 12:11). The power of the blood and the power of testimony work together in the task of overcoming the enemy. And they serve as more than just defense - the blood and the testimony are the offense we need to possess all that was purchased for us in our great salvation.

We all agree that we overcome because of the blood, but I am not sure we understand the power of testimony. People may challenge your theology, but they have no answer for your testimony. The testimony stands as your story of God's dealing in your life and serves as a powerful defensive or offensive weapon. It is unassailable because your testimony is connected to the dealings of God throughout history.

A few years ago while ministering in Oaxaca, Mexico, we were taken to a meeting in a run-down rehabilitation center overflowing with deeply disturbed people. The atmosphere appeared dark and foreboding and as the meeting progressed things got worse. Then it was my turn to speak and I knew that it was going to take more than words to break through. Just as I stood the Holy Spirit reminded me of the testimony I had heard of the miraculous salvation of a friend's father.

For all of his life David's father had been a disciple of Sai Baba, a Hindu guru. Even though all his sons had come to Christ and most served in ministry, he had never surrendered to the Gospel. A couple of years ago he was in the hospital in a coma. As David sat beside his bed one day, he began to cry out to God for the soul of his father and as he did he had a vision. It was as if he could see inside his father and, instead of healthy organs, what he saw was a twisted mass of insects, snakes and every kind of disgusting creepy crawler filling the whole inside of his dad's torso.

As he looked at the desperate condition of his father, he cried out to God, "What should I do?" And almost immediately he heard the Spirit say, "Plead the Blood." So, he began to plead the blood of Jesus over his father and as he did he saw one drop of blood fall from heaven and land on the chest of his father. From the point of impact *life* began to spread and replace death - the blood brought life. When the life of the blood reached his father's head, he suddenly woke up from the coma, and his first words were "David sing me a hymn." After David had sung a hymn or two, his father looked around the room and said, "Get rid of this rubbish," referring to all the pictures and paraphernalia related to his worship of Sai Baba.

The moment I began to share the story at the rehabilitation center the atmosphere in the room changed. At the end I gave an invitation and immediately things began to happen. Several responded for salvation. Two women who had been plagued by voices in their heads responded to a word of knowledge and were immediately healed. Testimony has the potential to change the atmosphere and usher in the presence and power of Jesus.

As soon as our leadership recognized what God was saying, we realized what we had been doing. When a healing would happen we would share the story and people would respond to the goodness of God. But in time we would forget or neglect the testimonies and over the weeks less would happen. As soon as we began to give more attention to testimony in both the services and in our preaching, the cyclical pattern began to break and we entered a season of steady increase.

We faced a challenge as we began giving regular testimonies, we wanted to be authentic and honest in everything we said and did - with no hype. So, if nothing happened in the previous week, we felt false if we shared something that "wasn't fresh." In an attempt to walk in integrity we realized that we were robbing the body of nutrients they needed to thrive. Testimonies have an unlimited "shelf life!" David shared testimonies hundreds of years old right along with recent ones (Ps. 78). All God has done builds us up for what He wants to do. We began to share at least one testimony every week. If we didn't have one in house, we would find one somewhere to share. We learned through this season that consistency in sharing testimonies requires understanding more about the value of the testimony.

THE VALUE OF TESTIMONY

David had a powerful grasp on the importance of testimony, and in Psalms 119 he gives several key insights into his understanding of how they could be used. First, he equates the testimonies of God's dealings in his life with riches. He writes, I have rejoiced in the way of Your testimonies, as much as in all riches (Ps. 119:14). The testimony to David held more value than wealth! Why? The Hebrew word testimony means continuance, still or again. The root word means "to repeat" or "to do again."[1] The word implies that anything God has ever done He is able and willing to do again. When you speak out a testimony, it has the power to reproduce itself. Another part of the definition carries the idea of "continuance of past events with the idea of repetition and permanence."[2] Absolutely stunning! *Everything God does becomes part of the permanent record of what He is willing to do again!*

John tells the church that the testimony of Jesus has a prophetic element ... *the testimony of Jesus is the spirit of prophecy* (Rev. 19:10). The prophetic speaks things into existence based on what God has done and what He has said. Through the testimony, the miracle has the power to repeat itself. So the testimony not only brings glory to God, it releases His goodness to do it again. Every testimony shared is filled with prophetic potential.

Jerrica, one of the young mothers in our church suffered a broken neck in a terrible car accident. Miraculously, as the result of a lot of prayer, God not only spared her life, but she recovered with no paralysis. The lingering effect was that her neck was bent slightly forward, her muscles were weak and she had limited motion. Jerrica is a worshiper and often uses flags during the service. After she got out of the hospital, she continued to worship, but it was a challenge with the posture brace she had to wear.

Two years later during a Randy Clark conference, a word of knowledge came for neck trauma in one of the services, and as she began to move her neck in obedience to the word, her neck popped so loudly that people around her heard it. Then she felt fire in the back of her head and neck and the stiffness was gone and full movement was restored. The orthopedic doctor that had been working with her was in the service and checked her out and was able to confirm the miracle.

Not long after this had happened I was in a meeting in Mexico and had just started to give her testimony when I heard the Spirit prompt me to have anyone with neck problems to stand before I shared the story. Three people stood and I told the story. In fact as you read this next testimony, if you have any issue with your neck, put your hand on your neck as you read the next paragraph and let the power of testimony touch you.

As soon as I had finished giving the testimony, I asked those standing to check out their necks and to their amazement two of the three who stood were healed before we prayed for them. And the third person standing, the pastor of the church, received his healing as those who stood around him laid hands on him. Testimony is pregnant with possibility and one of the works of the Holy Spirit is to empower testimony for repetition. Now, check yourself! See if you can do now what you couldn't do before.

TESTIMONY GIVES COUNSEL

Testimonies are powerful because they give us counsel from the spiritual realm. If we find ourselves uncertain what to do in a situation we face, by referring to a testimony of what God has done, faith will be released to see beyond the circumstances. Several of our young people enjoy praying for the sick on the streets. Often before the prayer they will give a testimony of someone healed from a similar situation or condition. It stirs faith in them and creates expectancy in the individual being prayed for.

David had the answer for dealing with natural counsel. He writes that *Thy testimonies also are my delight; they are my counselors* (Ps. 119:24).

Testimonies were a delight to him; he rehearsed them and meditated on them. But to David they served as more than good stories. He learned that he could go to the testimony for counsel, even to find God's will for a situation.

Remember the story of David and Goliath. David came into the camp to bring supplies to his brothers and heard Goliath blaspheming the God he loved. He heard the taunts but also the challenge and his heart responded. He was not focused on his ability but on the immense size of the God he worshipped. When he approached Saul, the natural counsel he received told him he couldn't do it. Saul gave him all the reasons: you are not big enough, experienced enough or strong enough. I love David's response. One day a bear came to destroy my sheep and I killed it. Then another time a lion came after the sheep and I killed it as well. And this Philistine will be no different! (1 Sam. 17:34-38). What did David do? He went to the testimony!

All that the king told him may well have been true, but the testimony of the lion and the bear told a different story. By recounting the testimony, he was able to overcome negative counsel and defeat the enemy. He overcame by the word of his testimony. David walked out of Saul's presence armed only with what he knew worked, because he held on to the testimony.

The good testimony generated faith to do more and go further. Testimony reproduces itself but is not limited by the specifics of the past experience. Neither the lion nor the bear compared directly with fighting Goliath; however, they set the stage to go further. Testimony catapults us further than we could ever go on our own. There is no limit to God's willingness to move through us. And if we let testimony direct us, God will do abundantly more than we could ask or think. That means that what he wants to do is unlimited by anything we have experienced, although it is fully supported by all He has done.

We love to study revival history, because anything God has done, He is willing and able to do again and even more. History helps us understand the dynamics that birth moves of the Spirit of God, as well as, things that hindered some of those same moves. But for me during these last few years, I have asked the Holy Spirit to help me find the testimony of those things that help us learn how to sustain the life of the Spirit. We want to learn to live in continuous revival so that it becomes an awakening. And as we meditate on the amazing works of God in history, we become bold in declaring what He wants to do and will do in our day.

TESTIMONY BRINGS BOLDNESS

David found great boldness in the testimonies of God's deliverance in his life. He writes, *I will also speak of Thy testimonies before kings, and shall not be ashamed* (Ps. 119:46). He understood that boldness comes when we give testimony of the things God has done for us. Are you feeling intimidated by a situation? Begin to rehearse the testimonies of God at work, and a fresh boldness will begin to come into your speech. The word witness comes from the same root as the word testimony. The boldness to witness is directly related to our willingness to hold on to the testimony of all God has done and is doing.

Tommy Hicks went to Argentina in 1954[3] to replace another evangelist who was unable to fulfill his commitment for a series of meetings. Tommy had very little time to prepare for the trip, but on the plane he had an encounter with the Holy Spirit who gave him both the name of a person that would help him (Peron) and the size stadium that should be rented. He asked one of the stewardesses if she knew someone named Peron, and she said, "Yes, he's the president of the nation."

On his arrival Hicks met with the committee that had invited him and told them he wanted to rent a large stadium. They laughed at him. The Evangelical church in the nation at the time was small and previous attempts to gather large crowds had failed. Undaunted, Hicks went to see the president. When he arrived at the building where the government offices were located, armed guards stopped him and asked what he wanted. Tommy explained that he wanted to hold an evangelistic and healing crusade. After a few more questions, one of the guards asked if God could heal him and Tommy immediately said yes. The man had been suffering from hepatitis and was in severe pain. Tommy took his hand and, as he prayed for the man, the pain left and he was completely healed. He looked at Hicks and told him, "Come back tomorrow and I'll get you in to see the President."

The next day when he arrived the guard immediately took Hicks and his interpreter in to see Peron. After explaining to the president his desire to have an evangelistic healing crusade complete with radio advertising, Peron asked if God could heal him. For several years he had suffered with a skin condition that had become so bad that he was not allowing any pictures of himself to be published. Tommy took his hand and, as he prayed, the power of God touched his body and in front of all he was completely healed. (God, give us boldness to speak Your word knowing that You will confirm it with signs and wonders.)

The power of God had opened the door and Peron gave Tommy everything he asked for. They began the meetings in the twenty-five thousand seat Atlantic Stadium, which was soon filled to capacity. The healing crusade was then moved to the much larger Hurricane Football Stadium that was quickly filled with hungry people. One newspaper reported that crowds of 200,000 people packed into the stadium and surrounding streets looking for a touch from God. Over the next two months, thousands were healed with many outstanding miracles, and over 300,000 made decisions for Christ. Tommy's boldness and the testimony of a guard unlocked a nation to the healing power of the gospel.

TESTIMONIES CREATE FAITH

David referred to the testimonies when he needed insight, but they were much more than just insight; they became his meditation. David said, *I have more insight than all my teachers, for Thy testimonies are my meditation* (Ps. 119:99). For David the testimonies of all God had ever done never got far from his thinking. And because they were held so close, they had profound influence over his actions. All the wisdom in the world cannot replace the testimony of what God has done for you.

The testimony of God's activity in the earth becomes our teacher – we learn what He is willing to do from what He has done. El Shaddai – the God who is willing and able to circumvent his own natural laws revealed Himself to Abraham and Sarah by making the impossible normal. They had a son well beyond childbearing years (Gen. 17:1). The more we see God do in and through our lives, the more our faith and expectancy will grow. God wants to do more than we can yet think or imagine. We get there by allowing what he has done to increase our faith for more.

On the first trip I made to Brazil with Randy Clark, I had a specific desire to see blind eyes open! For over a year I had prayed for every blind person I found and had no success. On the first night in Brazil I had a word of knowledge for a blind right eye and watched as someone came forward and received their healing. Even though I didn't get to pray for that person, my faith grew. Night after night I saw the blind receive their sight; then a few nights later I saw my first blind eye open! Confidence grows as we see God move and our faith grows, taking us from glory to glory with each release of God's power.

On one of the last nights of the trip I was part of the prayer team that was ministering with Carter Wood. Just before he started to speak, he asked all those who were terminally ill to come over to the right side of the platform and asked us to pray for them as he ministered. Just over a dozen came forward and immediately we began to see some of the most dramatic healings I had ever witnessed. Tumors disappeared, cancer was healed, blind eyes opened, and stroke victims were restored. For 20 minutes, as far as we know, everyone we prayed for was healed. At the end of the prayer time I was reeling. I knew I had just stepped into a place where I wanted to live. As I stood there I heard the Holy Spirit speak these words, "The impossible has finally become normal." After more than 40 years of ministry we are beginning to experience normal.

TESTIMONIES ARE OUR INHERITANCE

What is an inheritance? One of the ways inheritance is defined is "something from the past that is still important or valuable." The origin of the word is "to appoint an heir." So, someone becomes heir to something that has value. David writes, *I have inherited Thy testimonies forever, for they are the joy of my heart* (Ps. 119:111). He realized that as a child of God he became heir to all that God had ever done. When we grasp this, then every testimony becomes our inheritance. Everything God has ever done builds a solid foundation and all He has done becomes ours. The practical out-working of this is staggering. When we see a sick person, the first thing that should come to mind is a testimony. Often with a word of knowledge comes a testimony to reinforce what God is about to do. Testimonies are our inheritance and they have great value.

When Moses died, Joshua took responsibility to lead the people of God into the Promised Land. He had watched God do some amazing things through Moses and those miracles were his inheritance. But then it was his time and he needed his own testimony. As he prepared to take the people across the Jordan River, God gave him specific instructions so that a permanent testimony would be established, … *Take up for yourselves twelve stones from here out of the middle of the Jordan, from the place where the priests' feet are standing firm, and carry them over with you, and lay them down in the lodging place where you will lodge tonight* (Josh. 4:3).

In obedience to the word of the Lord, the next morning Joshua had the priests carry the Ark of Testimony, which represented the presence of God, ahead of the people. The Ark held the tablets of the law as the testimony of God's righteousness, the bowl of manna as testimony to God's provision and the rod of Aaron as a testimony to God-given authority. The ark as the testimony of all God had done now went ahead of the people to establish a fresh testimony for Joshua and all of Israel.

The moment the feet of the priests carrying the Ark touched the water it parted and they went and stood in the middle of the Jordan, allowing all the people of God to cross over. Then just as the Lord had commanded, they took twelve stones from the middle of the river and carried them on their shoulders out of the Jordan and set them up at Gilgal. There they became a permanent memorial to the hand of God at work in and through His people. Future generations would see that pile of stones and would remember what God had done for them. God's intention for this action was so *that all the peoples of the earth may know that the hand of the Lord is mighty, so that you may fear the Lord your God forever* (Josh. 4:24). It would be a reminder of what God had done and was still willing to do!

Gilgal became more than the first Israelite camp on the west of the Jordan River. It is where Samuel lived while he served as prophet and judge in Israel. It was where Saul was made King and it became one of the primary dwelling places of prophets in northern Israel. God had Joshua set up the testimony in a place where the prophetic spirit would keep the story alive. The word Gilgal means a "rolling wheel"[4] - a meaning consistent with the power of testimony. Remember that the Hebrew word testimony comes from the root "to repeat," or "to do again." The testimony of what God has done is not static; it has life in it. God does something powerful and wonderful, but it doesn't stop there! What He has done He is able and willing to do again. The 'life-cycle' of testimony is *repetition and permanence.*

Tucked into the narrative is another testimony that is easy to miss. The writer says, *Then Joshua set up twelve stones in the middle of the Jordan at the place where the feet of the priests who carried the Ark of the Covenant were standing, and they are there to this day* (Josh. 4:9). Joshua does something extraordinary; he added a piece to the obedience. He did exactly what God had asked him to do, but right in the middle of the river on the spot where the miracle happened he built his own memorial. He built it where nobody could see it, but he would remember it. Joshua built an altar of testimony in the middle of the Jordan, hidden from view but present as a testimony in his heart.

The commitment of Joshua to hang on to the testimony impacted me deeply. I realized how much of my personal testimony I had forgotten and I sat down and began to make a list of all the times I could remember that God had intervened in my life. As I was meditating on all He had done, I heard the Holy Spirit speak a powerful truth about testimony – *"If you remember the miracle, you will sustain the deliverance!"* How easy it is to forget what God has done for us. But if we are willing to hold on to the testimony, we will hold on to all that became ours through the miracle!

Every time we rehearse a testimony we remember God's goodness because every testimony declares that He is good. As we speak out the testimony we can expect God's goodness to be demonstrated in miraculous ways. This understanding of the incredible depth of the goodness of God is essential to keeping the fire of revival stoked in us.

keep the fire burning

CHAPTER FOUR

God's Goodness: Bedrock of Revival

'I Myself will let all of My goodness pass before you...'

Exodus 33:19

God is Good! Goodness is in His nature, making it inconceivable that He could be other than good. He never has a bad day; He is the very definition of good; He never gets in a bad mood. His goodness stands without measure and has no limits or defect. In fact the English word God comes from a Saxon word, which meant "The Good." It is fitting that the very definition of the word we use to describe God is so closely linked to His character of goodness. His goodness also extends to His acts so that all that He is and all that He does is good. Everything He does flows from Him as a manifestation of His goodness.

GLORY AND GOODNESS

One of the most profound requests in all of scripture comes in Exodus 33 where Moses asks God to show him His glory. Remember, this occurred after the miraculous deliverance from Egypt and the parting of the Red Sea. It comes after the pillar of cloud that guided the people of God during the day and pillar of fire that protected them by night. It falls after the whole of Mt. Sinai was shaken and covered with fire and smoke. Moses wasn't asking for another manifestation; He had witnessed the power of God, now he wanted to know who this God really was.

Two interactions set the stage for God's response to Moses. The first was Moses request *...let me know Your ways...* (Exod. 33:13). Moses wanted to know God better so that he could learn to please Him. Moses had seen God's acts; now he wanted to know His ways. The Hebrew word "ways" refers to the motives behind God's behavior. It includes the source of God's actions as well as understanding the way His power and authority are exercised. Moses wanted to get inside God's mind so that he could respond in the same way God did. This reminds me of Paul's request, "that I may know Him." Toward the end of his ministry Paul still wanted a deeper intimacy and revelation of the Savior he loved. This is how the mind of Christ operates for the believer. It allows us to respond in tune with heaven.

The second interaction began at the beginning of chapter 33 in which God offered to send an angel with them as they entered the land. From his relationship with God, Moses countered with an incredible statement of identity. He told God first that if His presence did not go with them, he didn't want to go. Then he follows in verse 16 by declaring that the presence of God served as the distinguishing mark of the people of God. The way the world would know God's people was by the manifest presence of God.

As we explore the goodness of God, these two interactions remain the primary issues in developing a revival culture. First, we need to know who God is so we can access His goodness for ourselves and for others. Second, we need to learn, as a people, to host His presence in such a way that we are marked and identified by the presence of God.

God's response to Moses' request to see His glory is breathtaking! *I Myself will make all My goodness pass before you, and will proclaim the name of the Lord before you...* (Exod. 33:19). Moses asked for glory; God responded by offering to show Moses all His goodness. Get that; God is going to reveal every facet of His inherent goodness to Moses. What a sight! God's goodness on display is a revelation of His glory. Fascinating, that the only man to get a glimpse of the glorious goodness of God came away from the experience with a radiant face! This revelation of God's goodness answers two desires: Moses' desire to please God and his desire for the presence of God. In revealing His goodness, God shows Moses that it is not as hard to please Him as he thought. The tablets of the law gave the children of Israel what not to do; now God revealed to them who He really was. I am good and full of goodness.

GOD IS GOOD

The goodness of God is a theme that runs throughout scripture. From Genesis to Revelation this foundational truth is reinforced. No single truth proves as pervasive. It is evident throughout the days of creation that everything God had spoken into being was good! It was good because it came into being as an expression of His nature. Man was His masterstroke, a being fashioned in His image and designed to express His nature. Then, with the creation of Eve, the plurality of God's image was perfected so that man and woman together could express His goodness as they ruled His creation.

Despite the ample testimony to the goodness of God and the abundant provision He had made for His creation, Adam and Eve proved vulnerable to an enemy looking for an opportunity to challenge the good nature of the God he had rejected. He came with a temptation that was crafted to question the goodness of God. Satan convinced Eve that somehow God was holding out on them. Why wouldn't He let them eat the fruit of this one tree? Man fell because they let their focus shift away from the goodness of God and onto the one thing that was prohibited. For a moment they doubted the goodness of God and the result was sin.

God's goodness is still under attack today. Because the enemy knows that if people ever truly saw how good God is, they would rush to Him for salvation. Satan still lies to believers today, tempting them to focus on something they think they need, while missing the overwhelming evidence of God's goodness all around them. For centuries the enemy has used religion as his tool to undermine the true nature of God. Religious legalism converts God's intention of relationship with the creator to a set of rules, which always give a distorted view of God.

Then, human efforts to explain or deal with circumstances outside of our control begin to attribute the work of the enemy to God, further undermining the truth of His goodness. This opens the door for deception that teaches that at any moment God may give people illness to make them a better person. Or perhaps He may make them poor to keep them humble. These kinds of distortions do not accurately reflect God's true nature. God is good and does not use sickness or poverty to discipline us. It simply is not in His nature.

Religion always reduces and restricts what we believe God can do or is willing to do. The legalism this creates, requires people to get right with God before He will touch them, but there is no basis for this in scripture or in experience. God loves people and is ready and willing to have them encounter His love and goodness so they can respond to Him. He will touch anyone willing to receive.

One morning two men were walking around on our Church property. Hannah, a teacher from our school, saw them and noticed that one had a new cast on his arm. She spoke with them and found out that he had just broken it. She asked permission to pray for him, and as she did, he felt a tingling sensation in his arm. A few minutes later the men left the property and the man's arm began to feel so much better that he went back to the doctor for a checkup. After the doctor examined him he removed the cast, because the arm was completely healed. One of the men later came to the church and confessed to one of the pastors that they were both wanted by the police and that the reason they had come to the property was to rob us. However, they were confronted with the goodness of God – a God so good that even though their motives were evil, He responded with goodness to heal the broken arm.

This revelation of the goodness of God powers the awakening. It challenges legalistic and religious norms and provides a key to freedom that the world has waited for. The world needs to understand that God is good and that He is in a good mood. The world desperately needs to know from us that His disposition exudes goodness, not anger.

AWAKENING TO HIS GOODNESS

How we view God is one of the most important components in sustaining the awakening. What image comes to mind when you think about God? Do we see Him as angry? Is there a feeling of foreboding when we think of entering His presence? Tozer says that, "What comes to your mind when you think about God ... is the most important thing about you." He goes on to say that, "We tend by a secret law of the soul to move toward our mental image of God."[1] This applies both individually and corporately. As individuals and as a church if we do not align with who He really is, it will prove very difficult to sustain a significant move of His Spirit.

This is still a central issue for the church. Doubting God's goodness keeps us from receiving and living in all He has for us. We sing that God is good, but I am not always sure we believe it. When we doubt His goodness, we lower our expectations of walking in His favor. Then, by attributing fickle human emotions to God, we are left with a distorted view of His nature.

The way we view God affects how readily we come into His presence. Quite simply we can't learn to host the presence of a God we do not believe is good. If we do not believe on the deepest level that He is good, we will be unable to come to Him when faced with temptation. Instead of letting the light of His presence cleanse us, we will tend to hide our sin and avoid His presence, running from Him rather than to Him after we have sinned. Adam and Eve hid from the presence because they lost sight of the goodness of God.

Just like Adam and Eve, we were created to live in the presence of God; in the fall we lost the right of access but not the ability. Within every human being is the ability to live in intimate relationship with God. The blood of Jesus purchased back the right to access the presence. As soon as the blood of the Son fell on the mercy seat, the Father tore the veil. His action gave us full permission to enjoy the presence we were created and designed for. Now we can come boldly to the throne of grace. "Face" is one of the literal meanings of the word presence. Because of Jesus we can stand in the face of the Almighty. We can look into His face and experience total acceptance from the Father who loves us.

This is crucial for awakening because His presence is the source of any move of God. Luke outlines the nature of a move of God. *Therefore repent and return, so that your sins may be wiped away, in order that times of refreshing may come from the presence of the Lord* (Acts 3:19). To experience the refreshing requires turning from one pattern of behavior to another; but look at its source! Refreshing comes from the presence of God. In fact refreshing can only be found in the presence – *Presence is the source!* You can live in continuous revival if you learn to live in and host the presence of God.

Our Christian school had a challenging year in 2011. There were conflicts and personality clashes in the staff and student body. In November during a conference Bill Johnson talked about hosting the presence of God and specifically asked how we would respond and live if the Holy Spirit, as a dove, rested on our shoulder. The next week at school one of the teachers printed off doves on white cardstock and the teachers cut them out and clipped them to their clothing as a reminder to host the presence.

The effect was immediate! The presence of God began to invade the school. The atmosphere changed as attitudes adjusted. Teachers and students became aware of His presence as they were drawn together. There was unity and peace within the staff relationships, but it also flowed into the classroom. The Spirit fell in the classroom, which made teaching difficult at times; joy and laughter even invaded the playground. Some of the chapels went on for hours with students all over the floor receiving from the presence of God. The teachers named that year, "The Year of the Dove." It was a wild year filled with laughter!! When we learn to host the presence of God, He changes the atmosphere. His presence in us flows through us and touches others around us.

When we understand and live in His presence, we discover His goodness and it becomes easy to trust Him. Once our hearts capture the glory of His goodness, confidence replaces timidity and faith replaces fear. Faith only grows in an atmosphere of knowing His goodness; otherwise, we draw back in uncertainty not really sure that God will come through. When we settle the fact that God is good and we can trust Him with our lives, we can surrender fully to His will and follow the leadership of the Holy Spirit. But - get ready - the deeper you delve into the nature of God the more goodness you will find.

GOD OF GRACE AND COMPASSION

When God displayed His goodness to Moses, He revealed one of His covenant names, the Lord God compassionate and gracious. The names of God are aspects of His nature and are expressed through His character. In revealing this new name to Moses, He was declaring for all time that compassion and grace are in His nature. God's goodness manifests to us as grace and compassion: grace - His response that covers our sin and continues to cover our weaknesses; *compassion* - His way of responding to us as we grow in Him, and as a way of responding through us in reaching out to others.

Our ability to understand and grasp this truth for ourselves has a lot to do with our impression of fatherhood. This image can also hamper us as we communicate God's nature to others. For years my ability to see the goodness of God was limited by the stern discipline of my father. He was a good man but a very damaged man, and the abuse he suffered made it easy for him to pass on the brokenness. Growing up, I had great difficulty seeing God as other than a stern taskmaster. My parents taught me to love God and I had surrendered my life to Him. But I had no real expectation of knowing Him intimately or interacting with Him other than through the scriptures. Prayer was even difficult, because I really didn't have much to say. I did my best to please God but felt in my heart that I was failing miserably.

Years later when I was baptized in the Holy Spirit I was shocked to discover that God talked. My whole view changed as I received a baptism of His love. I, for the first time in my life, stood in the presence of God secure in the righteousness of His Son. I delighted in the new identity that made me acceptable to the Father and in that realization the legalism of the past was replaced with a revelation of His grace and mercy.

I saw for the first time that in the act of revealing to Moses the law that would condemn, God gave a glimpse into His nature, a nature full of compassion and grace. Through His abounding goodness, He not only wants to demonstrate His goodness to us but also through us. So, how do we become one who receives His grace and compassion? How do we move from seeing God as angry and legalistic? We can begin by repenting of our fleshly efforts and receive His goodness expressed in grace and mercy. His promise to us is that He will be gracious and show compassion! Ask God for that baptism of love right now!

For us to grow in the miraculous, our faith must be linked to His grace and compassion, not our performance. God does not work through us because of our goodness but because of His. Miracles are not validations of our ministry but are expressions of God's grace and mercy as He extends His hand to demonstrate His goodness. Through believers receiving a revelation of the goodness of God and then allowing the Holy Spirit to move through them, signs, wonders and healings are being recognized and restored to the gospel message as vital components.

THE GOSPEL

The gospel is good news! In fact the old English meaning of gospel was "the good story." Every time the gospel was shared it came across as good news. *But when they believed Philip preaching the good news about the kingdom of God and the name of Jesus Christ, they were being baptized...* (Acts 8:12). The gospel is the good news not only because of the message of redemption; it is also good news because of our restored relationship with our good God. God so loved the world that He gave His Son (John 3:16).

Jesus demonstrated the heart of His Father. His life perfectly fleshed out the character traits of the Father. When His disciples asked Him if they could see the Father, He told them that if they had seen Him, they had seen the Father. The Father's love and the Father's goodness found perfect expression in every word and action of the Son.

After His ascension, the disciples appeared full of uncertainty until they were filled with the Spirit; then suddenly it all made sense. Their description of Jesus' purpose on earth shows they had a fresh understanding of the goodness of God expressed through Jesus. *You know of Jesus of Nazareth, how God anointed Him with the Holy Spirit and with power, and how He went about doing good and healing all who were oppressed by the devil, for God was with Him* (Acts 10:38). Jesus did on earth what a good God does. He went about demonstrating the goodness of God and destroying the works of the devil.

What Jesus did we are called to do. The goodness Jesus demonstrated is listed as a fruit of the Spirit. So, the Holy Spirit is working this same goodness into us. For us to preach the good news we must be convinced of the goodness of God to the point that it continually influences our actions.

Luke tells us that the good news is the good news of the kingdom - God's rule breaking into this time and space, displacing the rule of the enemy. He writes, *The law and the prophets were proclaimed until John. Since that time, the good news of the kingdom is being preached and everyone is forcing their way into it* (Luke 16:16). Jesus did what the law and the prophets could not do; He revealed the Father. The reign of terror was over and the good news was proclaimed. Look at the response to the presentation of the good news, "everyone is forcing their way into it." Wow! If this is not our experience, then perhaps we need to adjust our message. This had not been my experience until the last few years. But in meeting after meeting in Brazil I witnessed hundreds being healed by the power of God, and then when the invitation was given, people would run to the goodness of God they had just witnessed.

The gospel is good news because our good God made a way for salvation! The goodness of God loved us enough to send His son to die. His unconditional love and goodness is demonstrated as He washes us clean by the blood of Jesus, gives us a new nature, and transfers us from darkness to light. It is the goodness of God that puts His Spirit in us, marking us as His own, and brings us under His reign. It is the goodness of God that adopts us as His children and gives us a new identity – no longer an orphan! It is the goodness of God that transfers to us all the rights and privileges of sons and daughters as He takes His own ring of authority and puts it on our finger. It is the goodness of God that removes the grave clothes and gives us a robe of righteousness. And it is the goodness of God that heals our bodies, our minds and emotions. It is the goodness of God that puts His Spirit on us so that we can release His goodness to others. It is a revelation of the goodness of God that compels us to go out and touch others with His love.

GOODNESS AND REPENTANCE

In Paul's response to the Corinthian church he reveals one of his motivations for preaching the good news. He tells the church that because he knows and understands the fear of the Lord, he is compelled to persuade men and women to come to Christ. *Therefore, knowing the fear of the Lord, we persuade men...* (2 Cor. 5:11). The fear of the Lord to Paul served as a powerful motivation for evangelism. Hell and eternal judgment stand as undeniable truths of scripture. Those who don't receive Christ are doomed for eternity, because they have not accepted the sacrifice for sin paid by a Father so full of love that He gave His Son. However, as valid as the fear of the Lord serves as a reason to witness, it has limited value as motivator for conversion. Scaring people into heaven may well get decisions, but to become disciples people need to respond to a gospel message that displays His power and His love. People need to see the goodness of God so they can make the decision to give their lives to Him.

In fact just a few verses later he tells the church that in reality the love of Christ controls me (2 Cor. 5:13). Paul had the motivation to share the good news, because he knew the consequences of missing salvation. Yet, the message he preached was controlled by the love of God. His message contained so much of the love and goodness of God that people were captivated by it and drawn to repentance. Paul's message came wrapped in love and was presented with powerful demonstrations of the Father's goodness.

Only a revelation of God's goodness can break us free from our history, because it is His goodness that leads us to repentance (Rom. 2:4). We do not repent because we decide it is time. We repent because the goodness of God has been revealed to us in such a way that our hearts are captivated by His love and mercy. For the world today (jaded by every conceivable kind of teaching and deception) only a revelation of God's goodness through His church will alter the course of history.

A couple of years ago we spoke in a conference in Thailand and a group of pastors from Laos came over the border to the meetings. The man who led the delegation had been an official in the secret police several years before. His role had been to arrest and persecute Christians and he did his job well. At some point he became ill. One day after he had arrested a group of believers, the prisoners, seeing that he was sick, offered to pray for him. He let them and was immediately healed. The incident began to disturb him. "What kind of people would offer to pray for me while I am arresting them and what kind of God is this that would heal me while I am persecuting His people?" This encounter led to his conversion, followed almost immediately by imprisonment alongside those he had persecuted.

While in jail all he knew to do was what he had seen the other Christians do. So he prayed for the other prisoners and had many amazing encounters as God touched lives through him. Eventually, the jailor got so fed up with the disruption of normal, depressing jail life that he went to the authorities and told them it was too dangerous to have this man in jail. So they released him. From that time he has planted 50 churches - all of them built on the premise that we serve a good God – a God that wants to demonstrate His goodness by healing and setting people free even before they turn to Him.

Hosea prophesied, *Afterward... they will come trembling to the Lord and to His goodness in the last days* (Hosea 3:5). He looks forward to a powerful last days' revival that will be powered by a revelation of the goodness of God. The vision of this is absolutely stunning! Millions streaming, trembling to the goodness of God! Whole nations awakened to their Savior! Cultures transformed as they find new purpose - loving and serving our good God!

Today we can please God by displaying His goodness to the world! The ability and confidence to share His goodness with others is rooted in knowing our identity in Him. At the cross Jesus not only removed our sins, He made us new creations and adopted us into His family. Understanding and living in the rights and privileges of this new relationship are crucial to sustained revival.

CHAPTER FIVE

Identity: Gift of Righteousness

*Those who have received
...the gift of righteousness will reign in life...*

Romans 5:17

Identity is a paramount issue for creating and sustaining a revival culture in the local church. Most Christians really don't know their true identity in Christ and, historically, church culture has done little to remedy this failure. From around the middle of the fourth century, Christianity became the popular religion of Rome. This created an influx of marginally committed members into the church, who no longer did the work of ministry. To take their place, a professional clergy was needed to do the ministry, while the laity spent their energy in secular pursuits. This separation created a clergy/laity and a secular/sacred divide in the church. These false dichotomies fractured the body and altered what it meant to be Christian.

The awakening in the body of Christ that has begun to grow across the earth is powered by a realization that God has called every individual believer to minister. The advance of the gospel is dependent on each member of the church stepping into the revelation and recognition of their true identity in Christ. If people don't know who they are in God, they will never reach out in boldness and engage in sustaining a revival culture. If they don't know who they are, they won't access what they need to extend the kingdom. Finally, if the problem of lost identity is not addressed, believers will continue to spend their lives trying to become who they already are.

For us at Dayspring, the greatest single shift toward creating a culture of revival came with understanding our identity. As individuals in the body moved from seeing themselves as simply sinners saved by grace to new creatures in Christ, it was as if the light came on. Through the gift of righteousness they began to move from just forgiven sinners to living free. They moved from seeing themselves as servants to understanding that they were sons and daughters of the King. Only as sons and daughters did they find the confidence to access the resources of heaven and learn to release heaven on earth.

God created man in His image and, with the exception of the need for a helpmate that He provided, man lacked nothing. In this state of perfection they had no sense of lack, no health issues, no financial issues and no relationship issues. Man and woman knew exactly who they were and what they had been created for. God had commissioned them to care for and rule in His creation.

IDENTITY LOST

All this changed when they doubted God's goodness. In a moment of weakness they ate from the "tree of knowledge." The consequence of that decision plunged them into an identity crisis. They lost their bearings and no longer knew their purpose. Life then became a search to find that lost identity. We see this confirmed at the "Tower of Babel" where they were hoping to make a name for themselves (Gen. 11:4).

Webster defines identity in two ways: First, "The condition or fact of being the same or exactly alike," and second, "The condition or fact of being a specific person, individuality." Both parts of the definition mirror exactly what happened in the fall. Adam and Eve lost more than a place in the garden; they lost their identity. They exchanged an exact likeness with the Creator for individuality driven by a carnal nature. Paul describes this exchange when he describes the fallen nature of man. He says that they ... *exchanged the Glory of the incorruptible God for an image in the form of a corruptible man...* (Rom. 1:23). The exchange Adam and Eve made proved catastrophic to their identity in four specific ways.

First, they gave up their fellowship with God. They lost their access to the Father along with the relationship of intimacy they had enjoyed with their Creator. In exchange they lived with broken fellowship, distance, and hiding. The introduction of sin erected a veil between God and man that remained in place till the death of Christ. They could remember the intimacy they had lost but were powerless to regain it. Regret, remorse, condemnation and guilt crept into their fractured relationship with their Creator.

Second, Adam and Eve were created with a perfect nature. Their attitudes, thoughts and motives mirrored God's. But when they fell, their God-like nature was replaced with a carnal nature - filled with self-will, self-centeredness and individuality. This separated them from God and from each other. Their minds, once holy, now began to be filled with thoughts of rage, jealousy, resentment and bitterness. They had never known depression, sadness, brokenness or loss, but now these unfamiliar thoughts swirled through their minds.

Third, in Eden, God made His resources fully available to Adam and Eve. He provided for them abundantly so they could prosper. No sickness could touch them and everything they needed for health was provided. God even included a "tree of life" that would have extended their lives indefinitely. The consequence of sin drove them out of this place of full provision and into a realm of lack. Hard work, thorns, weeds and unyielding ground replaced the lush fruitfulness of the garden. In this unfamiliar harsh environment, provision came from self-effort combined with sweat and toil. Bodies accustomed to living in health now began to experience infirmity, pain and disease. The more difficult life became the more they longed for the supernatural provision they had lost.

Fourth, they were created with purpose. In creation man and woman were designed and commissioned to rule in God's creation. Every day they walked in the power and authority God had delegated to them. In the fall God's mandate to rule and subdue was abdicated and mankind stepped into a realm ruled by elements beyond their control. They exchanged pursuing their God-given purpose for an aimless search for meaning. Their goal shifted from dominion to survival as their days filled with the struggle to stay alive.

PROMISE OF REDEMPTION

Before creation, God had already planned redemption. So in the moment of dealing with the consequence of sin, God provided a promise of restoration (Gen. 3:15). A deliverer would come through their descendants who would crush the head of the serpent and reverse the effects of the fall. As a shadow of this redemption God initiated a covering, replacing the fig leaves of self-effort with the skin of an animal. Throughout the Old Covenant, God mandated the shedding of blood to provide temporary relief from the consequences of sin. While all creation waited, looking forward to the day that the Savior would be born.

When the time was fulfilled God sent His Son to initiate His plan of redemption. Jesus lived a perfect life before the Father, free of the effects of the fall. He was secure in His identity and had unhindered fellowship with the Father. Although tempted, He lived free from sin – a demonstration of the new nature. Having fulfilled all righteousness, He lived under an open heaven with all resources available to Him, and with perfect obedience He lived only to fulfill the will of His Father. His death and resurrection made available to us freedom from the old and abundant life purchased with His blood. All that Adam lost can be found in Jesus!

RESTORATION OF RELATIONSHIP

Within our God-given design lies the spiritual capacity to have fellowship and intimacy with the Father. Sin erected a barrier but, in the moment of Christ's death, His blood paid the price for our redemption. The Father tore the veil of the temple from top to bottom, inviting us back into fellowship with Him. Christ, the perfect sacrifice, paid the price and forever satisfied God's justice. As a gift of grace God has justified us, allowing us unhindered access to His presence. We have been invited to *draw near with confidence to the throne of grace* (Heb. 4:16). And we can come boldly, because we stand complete in His righteousness.

In the instructions for constructing the Ark of the Covenant, God told Moses to build a mercy seat as a covering. It would be a place where the blood of the sacrifice would be poured out. God goes on to tell Moses they could meet there at the mercy seat (Exod. 25:22). The word *meet* used here also means agree or to come into agreement. Catch the implication. As God looked across the mercy seat, He would see Moses through the blood of the sacrifice. In this place of grace God would see Moses through the righteousness of the Son, not based on his performance.

With the mercy seat in place and fellowship restored, we become partakers of the full benefit of our inheritance in Christ. Understanding our new identity moves us beyond forgiveness of sins to see ourselves as transformed. Through God's dynamic act of recreation we have been redeemed from the law and adopted as His children. We can now come to God not as beggars but as sons and daughters.

Philip is our son; he lives near us and has a key to the back door. When he comes in, he doesn't need to knock or ask permission; he has free access to our house. Many things have vanished from our refrigerator through the years because our son has free access to that as well. Not only that, he has a key to the garage where we keep all the tools. He can come any time of day or night and take what he needs to do a job. He thinks like a son, not a hired hand.

Then there is our friend Ronnie. Ronnie often does work for us; he trims the hedges, rakes the leaves and helps us around the house. When Ronnie needs something, he comes to the back door and knocks, waiting politely for us to answer. He doesn't just walk in. His access to our home and my garage is limited to what he needs to fulfill his responsibilities. If he asks for something, we usually let him have it or use it, but it is very different from the relationship we have with our son.

The challenge for us as believers is to learn to approach the Father from a position of family, rather than outsider. Too many believers have received forgiveness for their sin but have never walked in the privilege of their restored relationship. Paul tells us that we have received a spirit of adoption (Rom. 8:15). This means that a primary role of the Holy Spirit is to help us understand and walk in our new identity. This work of the Spirit serves as an essential foundation for creating a revival culture. To host the presence of God in our daily walk, we must take full advantage of the fresh access and intimacy to the Father He has offered.

RESTORATION OF NATURE

We were all born with a sinful nature. As a result of Adam's sin we inherit this nature as a fundamental part of our fallen identity. Without redemption, there is no escape from the consequences of our inherent sinfulness. Christ's sacrifice offers us a new birth and the opportunity to live with a new identity. This identity comes complete with a new restored nature purchased with Christ's blood.

The law stands as God's perfect standard, but it has no power to give life or grace. Christ died, having fulfilled the righteous demands of the law. Jesus *is the end of the law for righteousness to everyone who believes* (Rom.10: 4). By accepting Him, the Law of God is fulfilled in us and written on our hearts (Ps. 40:8). We are a new creation, new creatures in Christ; the old has gone the new has come! (2 Cor. 5:17). Paul tells the Ephesians to *be renewed in the spirit of your mind, and put on the new self, which in the likeness of God has been created in righteousness and holiness of the truth* (Eph. 4:24).

Catch the implication here! The new self is created in the "likeness of God." In the new birth the image of God has been restored in our nature. We receive the mind of Christ so that we can think like Him, react like Him and love like Him. In fact the work of ministry is to see Christ formed in every believer. So, what is the problem? Why do so few believers truly represent Christ in their daily lives? We believe most fail to recognize they are a new creation.

The chief weapon the enemy uses to keep us from walking in the fullness of our new identity in Christ is condemnation. If he can keep us feeling bad about ourselves, he can keep us ineffective and self-focused. If we don't know who we are, we listen to the lie and think of ourselves as less than what Jesus paid for. We see ourselves as sinners saved by grace but not as new creatures in Christ. We know that we are forgiven, but we don't believe we are free.

This was the issue that Paul addressed with the Romans, *are we to continue in sin that grace might increase* (Rom. 6:1). The problem with this question was that they didn't see themselves as changed; only forgiven. This does not diminish forgiveness but helps us realize that without change we will get caught in a never-ending cycle of repentance. We celebrate the grace that forgives, but we are to live in our new identity, glorying in the grace that changed us. Paul's next question makes this clear, *How shall we who died to sin still live in it?* (Rom. 6:2). He needs them to understand that a profound change came about in their salvation. He then answers his own questions by laying out the process of embracing our new identity.

First, to understand the new nature purchased for us, we must identify with His death (Rom. 6:3, 4). We were baptized into His death, which means that when He died, we died. Not only that, but in that act there was a circumcision - the removal of the flesh – the old nature was cut out (Col. 2:10-14). *Knowing this* - the prolonged form of the verb "to know" means (to know absolutely) (Rom. 6:6). We must know absolutely *that our old self was crucified with Him, that our body of sin might be done away with....* We are no longer slaves to sin, because *he who has died is freed from sin* (Rom. 6:7). Time to believe it!

Second, we must identify with His resurrection. When Christ was raised, we too were raised from the dead, but now with a new nature. As we identify with His resurrection we become a new creature in Christ (2 Cor. 5:17). His resurrection life creates a new nature in us. Paul tells the Ephesians to *...put on the new self, which in the likeness of God has been created in righteousness and holiness of the truth* (Eph. 4:24). Because our new nature is made in His likeness, it becomes natural to take on the mind of Christ. As we realize the significance of this transformation, we see a restoration of our mind and thinking patterns. Our new nature has no inclination to sin; our new nature wants to be in alignment with God's will and purpose; the new nature has no resistance to the work of the Holy Spirit. The greatest joy of our new nature is the restored intimacy with the creator. Believe it; the old is gone and all things have become new.

Third, we must learn to think correctly. *Even so, consider yourself dead to sin* (Rom. 6:11). The word "consider" here means to gather up all the facts and make a decision.[1] His death is my death; I died with Him so I am dead to sin. His life is my life, so I am alive in Him with a new nature. *Therefore, do not let sin reign* (vs.12). Don't let sin exercise power over you any longer - it is dead in you and you are dead to it. *Don't go on presenting your members to unrighteousness* (vs.13). Don't even think of yourself as unrighteous. We have died to sin and are now alive to righteousness (1 Pet. 2:24).

In other words, if we want to change actions, we must change thinking. If we learn to think correctly about our new nature, our feelings will follow and we will begin to feel free. And if we think and feel correctly, godly actions will follow. Correct actions result from correct thoughts. We are told to present ourselves as alive from the dead and as instruments of righteousness because, *Sin shall not be master over you* (vs.14). Believe that the old nature is dead, act like the old nature is dead, and you will begin to live life as a new creation in Christ.

Finally, ask yourself a question. If we are dead to sin, why do we have so much trouble with it? Well, let me answer with a question of my own. Why does a rattle snake bite? The answer could be that they feel threatened, but behind that is a simple explanation - striking their prey is in their nature. You can try to tame the snake, counsel it, educate it, and treat it with favor but in the end it still bites because it is in its nature. The only way to keep a snake from biting is to kill the snake. You will not get free from your sin nature by any other means than dying to that part of you. Stop resurrecting your old nature! Decide today that you are dead to it. You may well have to do it daily as Paul suggests, but just do it!

RESTORATION OF RESOURCES

Christ lived perfect before the Father, demonstrating a life lived fully in the new nature. He had unhindered fellowship with the Father and, although tempted, He lived free from sin. As the Son of Man full of the Holy Spirit, He fulfilled all righteousness. At His baptism heaven opened over Him and the Father confirmed His identity. He lived and ministered under an open heaven with all resources of heaven available to Him. With His death and resurrection, He made available to us abundant life through our new nature.

One of the articles kept in the Arc of the Testimony was the bowl of manna (Exod. 16: 33). The manna was kept as a testimony of God's supernatural provision for His people. Remember that a testimony is a reminder of what God has done but also a promise of what He is willing to do again. With Jesus' blood now on the mercy seat, supernatural provision is available to the people of God.

God's original intention was that His people prosper and be in health. If we understand that supernatural provision comes as an integral part of being in Christ, then we will live in abundance that is not based on performance, but on His grace. If we depend solely on our own work ethic for our provision, then our ability to provide becomes our source. Our provision comes from our strength, our mind, our ability and is limited by what we have available.

But supernatural provision comes from a different source. We are told that, if *we seek first the kingdom of God and His righteousness* (Matt. 6:33), everything we need will be provided. What is required is for us to shift our focus to living in a reality of the rule of God in our lives. He becomes our source. I don't know about you, but I want to learn to have my source in Him and not in my ability.

As we come to understand our new identity, we realize that we have become a joint-heir with Christ. In Him there is abundance and if we are in Him and related to Him through the new birth, then we can live in the same provision and abundance that He experienced. God gives abundance so that we can supply for others (2 Cor. 8:14). We need to have, *abundance for every good deed* (2 Cor. 9:8). We are even told that, *He who has abundance shall have more* (Matt. 13:12). The church in this move of God must step out of the poverty mentality and into a time of abundance so that the work of God can move forward as God intended. Abundance is not to prove our spirituality or to live in luxury, but so that the goodness of God can be fully displayed to the world. He wants to give us access to the resources of heaven!

On my first trip to Brazil I saw blind eyes open for the first time. A few weeks after that, I was in Sri Lanka and fully expected to see God move in a similar way. During one of the sessions, I felt impressed to ask anyone with eye problems to come forward. I expected a handful but about 30 came forward. I felt fairly confident in praying for an individual but this was different. As I walked to the end of the line to begin praying I asked for direction on how to minister and saw a mental impression of a refrigerator in heaven. Then it opened and I saw that it was full of eyeballs! So, as I prayed for each person I simply reached up, took an eyeball from the refrigerator, and placed it in the eye in front of me.

When I had finished, we began to get the testimonies of what had happened and the results were amazing. Several who had needed glasses could now see clearly without, but the most astounding testimony came from a father. He brought his son to the front and had him read from the bible to show that he was healed. Then he told us that his son's eyesight had been so poor that he had been unable to see to learn to read. It took a few moments for this to sink in - in that moment the son had not only received his sight but also had sovereignly learned to read.

A few months later we traveled to Lebanon and I gave the testimony of the eyes being healed. Toward the end of the conference we spent time activating the leaders to pray for healing. One of the pastors was praying for a man who had a birth defect in his heel which made walking diffi-cult; he had never been able to put weight on it. After praying a couple of times nothing much had changed, but after the third prayer, I heard the man being prayed for exclaim that his leg had become cold and instantly all the pain had left. He could put full weight on it.

Later, I was talking to the pastor who had prayed for him to get the full story. He said that after the first two prayers and no change, he asked God what to do and saw a picture of a refrigerator. When he opened it, there was a leg inside; so he took it out and stuck it on the man he was praying for. It was at the exact moment the man's leg got cold and the healing manifested. God has a sense of humor!

RESTORATION OF PURPOSE

Jesus submitted to John's baptism in order to fulfill all righteousness (Matt. 3:15). Even though John objected, Jesus had come for a purpose that could only be accomplished if He fulfilled every aspect of the law. From the day He was born His parents took Him to the temple and did with Him all that was required in the law. He would now begin His ministry, but not without receiving a baptism from John. He couldn't begin to minister unless He had fulfilled all righteousness. God answered from Heaven announcing that, *this is My beloved Son, in whom I am well pleased* (Matt. 3:17).

Jesus did not come to abolish the law but to fulfill it (Matt. 5:17). As the Son of Man, He lived obedient to God's law, demonstrating the power of a Spirit-filled life. He stood at the end of His time here on earth completely righteous before the Father. He went to the cross as a perfect sacrifice totally acceptable to God. Through this obedience, He is able to gift us with His righteousness that meets God's approval. ... *Much more those who receive the abundance of grace and of the gift of righteousness will reign in life through the One, Jesus Christ* (Rom. 5:17).

Staggering! Jesus has made His righteousness available to us as a gift. The effects of sin are reversed as a gift from God! We have received an abundance of grace; we have also received the gift of righteousness. Now in this life we can reign! The commission to rule given Adam and Eve is restored to us in Christ!

In creation God gave man and woman the responsibility of ruling in His creation and subduing anything that would seek to disrupt God's purpose. In the death and resurrection of Jesus, He took back the authority that had been lost in the fall and now offers it to any who would step up and take responsibility for extending His rule. In the great commission Jesus told His disciples that He had all authority back in His hand and then commissioned them to go in the power of the Spirit and the authority of His commission and fulfill His purpose on the earth.

As a church and as individuals we must learn to live in the revelation of the gift of righteousness. Our new identity comes complete with restored fellowship with the Father. We can host His presence. Our new identity restores our nature so that we can respond as heaven responds. And our new identity comes complete with all the resources needed to fulfill our purpose. Jesus …*went about doing good and healing all who were oppressed by the devil* (Acts 10:38). That is exactly how we should live our lives.

Until we understand who we are as royal sons and daughters of God, we spend our lives trying to earn what He has freely given us. This robs us of the confidence to step into the greater works that Jesus promised (John 14:12). Countless believers never move into personal revival because they lack a revelation of the miraculous living hope they received as part of their new identity.

CHAPTER SIX

Hope: Living With Expectancy

His great mercy has caused us to be born again to a living hope…

1 Peter 1:3

A culture of revival is an optimistic atmosphere filled with hope. In a world surrounded by bad news, hope looks into the eternal nature of God and finds a place of confidence and safety. *This hope we have as an anchor of the soul, a hope both sure and steadfast and one which enters within the veil* (Heb. 6:19). Hope has power because its source comes directly from relationship with the Creator. Instead of looking at the circumstances, hope turns to look into the face of God and takes strength from adoration and intimacy.

I remember the first time I saw an anchor. I was traveling with my parents on the way to Africa and we stopped at a port somewhere in the Mediterranean. My father and I got off the ship and saw, lying on the dock in front of us, an anchor with a massive chain attached. I am sure part of my memory has to do with being 10 years of age, but it was awesome - the biggest, strongest thing I had ever seen. Every time I think of hope this is the picture that comes to mind. We have a hope as strong as that anchor. And the anchor is firmly set in the very presence of God, absolutely secure. Even better, I see that massive chain connected to my heart and I am being drawn irresistibly into His presence. Hope is alive; it is active and it is real.

CURE FOR PESSIMISM

Hope is the antidote to pessimism. This means that a revival culture must be filled with hope, because revival and pessimism can't cohabitate. In the presence of difficulty, hope finds confidence in the character of God ... *we may have strong encouragement, we who have fled for refuge in laying hold of the hope set before us* (Heb. 6:18). Hope is a hiding place; not a "head in the sand" denial of what is going on but a redirection of our attention to find the truth!

I like the idea of "strong encouragement." It gives a hint that there is more available in hope than we realized. The phrase *laying hold of* comes from a single Greek word that means - to take power over, to become powerful, or to be master over. When we turn our focus from the situation and take hold of hope, we receive power to deal with the circumstance. Hope makes us master over the powers that are not in alignment with the will of the King.

Sharron grew up in an active Christian family and accepted Christ at a young age, but for several years she had just been going through the motions. She became very interested in current events, politics in particular, and most days watched cable news morning till evening. She was well informed on the issues but becoming increasingly frustrated and hopeless. One evening she got desperate and began repenting of complacency. The presence of God came into the room and she asked the Holy Spirit to "ride my case where I need it; I didn't want to be a dead Christian anymore!"

The next morning she went to turn on the news and heard the voice of the Lord say, "Don't turn it on." She pulled her hand back; then He said, "I'm on the throne and no one is taking it from Me!" She didn't turn the news on that day and instead started streaming worship music into their home. In the two years since the shift in her focus she has been able to stop complaining about the government and has started praying for our leaders instead. The shift of focus brought an increase of His presence into their home that has spread to many others, and she has now become a carrier of revival in Dayspring,

Hope is such a pervasive theme in scripture that the word occurs 140 times, split almost equally between the Old and New Testaments. This is because hope provides the primary protection for our minds. Paul tells the church, *But since we are of the day, let us be sober, having put on the breastplate of faith and love, and as a helmet, the hope of salvation* (1 Thess. 5:8). The hope of salvation keeps our minds focused, protects our thoughts and keeps us free from fear. Without hope we are subject to the swirl of life around us. But with hope we are protected from the storm.

The word *hope* carries both the idea of expectation and anticipation. So hope is a joyful and confident expectation of good. Hope also means to anticipate with pleasure. In a society where everything thrown at us is negative, this is profoundly important. For Christians in this hour many of the voices we listen to and trust present a pessimistic perspective that promotes fear and disbelief. These negative influences are deadly for revival. The faith we need is dependent on the hope within us. Faith after all is *the substance of things hoped for* (Heb. 11:1). To have faith you need hope! Without a hope-filled view of what God is doing in the earth, we lack the faith to release the miracles.

Many in the church see regular healings and miracles. Almost without exception those moving with the greatest effectiveness are those who refuse to be distracted by the negative around them. They focus on what God is doing in the earth. Only hope that has its anchor in the presence of God has the power to change our minds. Only in a place of hope will we be able to see and hear that heaven speaks. Only when we hear what heaven is speaking will we have the boldness to step out and release the power of the kingdom.

LIVING HOPE

All the patriarchs were people of hope; despite their circumstances they looked forward to the fulfillment of the promise of God even though they weren't experiencing it. Most died still looking forward to the promise of a Savior. *In hope against hope he believed, in order that he might become a father of many nations, according to that which had been spoken...* (Rom. 4:18).

We have the privilege of living on the other side of the promise. We don't have to wait for the Messiah; He has come. We don't have to live in the shadow of the law, because Jesus has fulfilled it and offered us His righteousness as a gift. As sons and daughters of the King we have access behind the veil and have been invited into a deep and personal intimacy with the Father. From that place of intimacy we hear His heart beat and embrace His perspective. Peter calls this a living hope.

A young couple in our church, Zach and Natalie had just found out they were pregnant for the third time. They set up a Doctor's appointment to make sure everything looked "normal," because the year before they had lost their second baby during pregnancy. When they had the ultrasound, the doctor could detect no heartbeat and the placenta was not forming properly. The child was dead in the womb. This would be their second miscarriage and they were devastated.

When they shared their story with me Sunday morning, my focus was on pastoring them in this difficult situation, and I called Sally over to help me. When I told her what happened, she reacted immediately and jammed her hand onto Natalie's stomach and yelled "Life! Life!" I was a little taken aback because it "wasn't very pastoral" but Natalie said that the moment Sally spoke life into her, she felt something change inside of her body.

The next day they set up an appointment to have another ultrasound. They were hopeful but very nervous and not quite sure what to expect. This time, however, they were in for a GREAT surprise! To everyone's delight the doctor detected the baby's heartbeat, and the placenta was now formed, making everything "normal." They had no other complications during that pregnancy and ended up naming their beautiful baby girl, Miracle, as a testimony of the miracle God had performed on their behalf. Since then, they have gone on to have three more healthy children and Natalie is now expecting baby number six.

Blessed be the God and Father of our Lord Jesus Christ, who according to His great mercy has caused us to be born again to a living hope through the resurrection of Jesus Christ from the dead (1 Pet. 1:3). The new birth changes our understanding of possibility. We were born again into a hope that is alive. This living hope is the life of Christ living and working in us. When Sally laid her hand on Natalie's stomach, she tapped into this living hope, which brought life into death! Our hope is alive!

The word living comes from the root *zoe* which in scripture refers to God's kind of life, the very life we receive at the new birth. We were dead in our sin until God gave us the gift of eternal life. This eternal zoe life is living on the inside of us and it is full of hope. Our thinking and our conduct changes when living hope rules in our lives. We begin to live from an eternal perspective. Natural barriers no longer bind us, because the hope in us is anchored behind the veil. The more we let living hope rule our thinking, the more clearly we see into the eternal purpose of God, and the less influenced we are by all that is going on in the natural realm.

ANCHORED HOPE

When we are born again, we pass from death to life and receive a living hope as our birthright. But, if it is ours as a birthright, why do so many struggle with hope? I think it is quite simple. If we are not careful, our hope gets fixed to the wrong things. Because of the nature of hope, it will always be anchored to something. Sometimes it is our ability, our gifts, or our performance. Some are fixated on personal happiness, while others put their trust in the economy, government, business, and the list goes on. One of the most common dysfunctional anchors is to fix our hope on a person – a spouse, a pastor or friends.

Hope becomes living when it is fixed on God. The Christian life works when Jesus becomes the anchor of every part of our existence. … *Fixing our eyes on Jesus, (the Anchor) the author and perfecter of faith…* (Heb. 12:2). When our hope is on Him, we are purified (1 John 3:3) and conformed to His image. When we look at Him, our perspective changes. We begin to see through His eyes and hope grows.

Remember one of the definitions of hope is expectation. The English word comes from the prefix "ex" meaning out and "spector" meaning to see. Expectation then is the ability to see out. Literally, when we have hope, we can see clearly outside or beyond our circumstances. This is what it says about Jesus …*who for the joy set before Him endured the cross, despising the shame, and has sat down at the right hand of the throne of God* (Heb. 12:2). Jesus had an expectation beyond the momentary suffering. His hope was anchored in the nature of His Father and the joy of their master plan of salvation.

LIFECYCLE OF HOPE

When Paul wrote to the Romans he described a pattern that increases our hope. I like to call it a lifecycle, because each time we walk through this scenario our faith increases, our love increases and the ability to sustain the presence increases. He began with the life we received at salvation. *Therefore having been justified by faith, we have peace with God through our Lord Jesus Christ...* (Rom. 5:1). By faith we receive His payment for sin and immediately see that God is not mad at us! We are no longer striving to please Him. We are at peace and have the privilege of full, unhindered access to Abba.

All this comes to us from Jesus, but there is more ...*through whom also we have obtained our introduction by faith into this grace in which we stand; and we exult in hope of the glory of God* (Rom. 5:2). We are introduced by faith to grace, a grace so powerful that it literally transforms us. Grace is not just favor; it is the power of the risen Savior living inside us, transforming us on the inside into His image. God's abundant grace is the cornerstone of our new identity.

The grace we stand on leads us to exalt in hope. Literally, boast in hope! Hope lets us access what is present reality in heaven and it even reaches into the future. Through hope, faith is not limited by experience. It gives us access to everything we were created for; it gives us access to our destiny. Hope lets us dream with God, who is ready to do more than we can even imagine. Through hope we break the limitations of the natural realm and begin to live in the supernatural realm where the impossible becomes normal. With this kind of hope faith comes naturally, because it is the substance of extravagant hope.

Yet it doesn't stop there! This lifecycle has another step. *And not only this, but we also exult in our tribulations, knowing that tribulation brings about perseverance...* (Rom. 5:3). Exalt in tribulations! No way; why did hope lead me here? Big dreams don't come into reality without pressing in. The root of the word tribulation is pressure. None of us like pressure but very little of value has ever been produced without it. Notice the word exalt, this speaks of more than merely enduring pressure, but of exalting God in the midst of it. Fixing our eyes on Jesus, we deeply love Him no matter what is going on around us. The highest praise is praise under pressure. And praise under pressure produces perseverance.

What is our response to pressure? If we stay flexible and focused on God and His grace (perseverance), then the pressure will produce growth (proven character). Paul goes on to say, and *perseverance, proven character; and proven character, hope...* (Rom. 5:4). Perseverance produces character and the growth in character produces more hope. The lifecycle of hope begins in grace, which increases hope. Hope grows as we dream beyond our ability; the big dream requires more faith that increases the pressure as we are being pressed into His image. The pressure increases our worship, releasing more grace, which increases our hope, causing the pressure of growth requiring us to access more grace... you get the idea.

Each cycle of this process ends in a fresh baptism of the Father's love *...and hope does not disappoint, because the love of God has been poured out within our hearts through the Holy Spirit who was given to us* (Rom. 5:5). Every time we respond correctly to pressure we experience more of the love of God poured out into us by the Holy Spirit and the more of His love we receive the more we give out. Revival culture grows on this outpouring of love. Hope does not disappoint – it will never make us ashamed. This is a call to dream big!

FIXED ON GRACE

To sustain under pressure, our hope must be fixed completely on grace. *Therefore, gird your minds for action, keep sober in spirit, fix your hope completely on the grace to be brought to you at the revelation of Jesus Christ* (1 Pet. 1:13). Prepare for action (pressure) by keeping our hope fixed completely on the grace - not on our past performance, not on the circumstances, and not on what others are doing. If we don't keep focused on the grace, hope will quickly disappear. Grace is the key to sustaining a life of living hope.

JOYFUL HOPE

This may not sound like a lot of fun, but the intention of the Father is that the whole process would be with such joy that we hardly notice the circumstances. Paul tells us that, *Now may the God of hope fill you with all joy and peace in believing, that you may abound in hope by the power of the Holy Spirit* (Rom. 15:13). Hope is in the nature of God; He is the God of hope. God, the author of hope, has so designed the process of our growth that it is always full of joy and peace. We are enabled to abound in hope by the power of the Spirit, because the power of the Spirit is always available to increase hope.

The Spirit of God helps us focus on God Himself - the source of hope - that empowers us to live full of joy and peace no matter what is going on around us. This lifestyle of joy and peace will begin to attract attention, giving us opportunity to share the source of our hope.

HOPE AND BOLDNESS

Living hope makes us incredibly bold. Paul says, *Having therefore such a hope, we use great boldness in our speech* (2 Cor. 3:12). If we want people to walk in boldness, we must introduce them to a living hope.

Remember when the early church came under pressure for the first time. When Peter and John were arrested, they responded by focusing on God's goodness and let worship and praise fill their jail cell. Worship in the midst of trials will turn our valley of trouble into a door of hope, (Hosea 2:15) a doorway that leads to joy and boldness.

After their encounter with the authorities, instead of laying low, they prayed for more boldness and an increase of the miraculous (Acts 4:29). When our hope is fixed on the eternal plan and purpose of God, and when it draws its life from intimacy with the Father, then the only possible response will be joy and boldness in the midst of difficulty!

HOPE AND CALLING

Accessing living hope is essential if we are to fulfill our calling. *I pray that the eyes of your heart may be enlightened, so that you may know what is the hope of His calling, what are the riches of the glory of His inheritance in the saints* (Eph. 1:18). This is written to the church and tells us that the eyes of our heart need to be opened. We need a revelation to see more than we see at present – turn the light on. Our calling and hope are connected; the more aligned we are with our calling, the more hope is available. In fact hope is hard to find if we walk away from our calling. Obedience to the call is a key to accessing hope, no matter what the call is. Business, teacher, engineer, pastor, missionary, parent – they all require obedience in order to access hope.

When we walk in our calling, we have access to our inheritance. Step outside of our calling and accessing the blessing becomes difficult. We can't live for self and live in our blessing. We are called as a son or daughter of the King, but the blessing of that calling only flows from relationship. The prodigal son had to return to his calling to reconnect with the blessing of abundance.

We are called as co-laborers with Christ, but notice that our inheritance is in the saints. We are designed to work together with the rest of the body; some of what I need is in you and some of what you need is in me. We will miss some of our hope if we don't value our relationships. The very people who produce some of our greatest pressure are part of our inheritance. Living hope is a daily perspective that guards our minds as we relate to others, for hope sees others through the eyes of Jesus. Looking through His eyes allows us to see their future rather than their past. This frees us from judgment and lets us see their destiny no matter how broken they appear.

HOPE ANTICIPATES

Remember that one of the words used to define hope was to anticipate. Anticipate is a combination of *ante* a prefix which means "before" and *cipare*, which means, "to take." Essentially to anticipate something means to take before or to take in advance. We have an amazing inheritance and through hope we have access to more than we have experienced. Through hope we can anticipate what God is doing and reach out and take it. Anticipating hope lets us grow past our experience because it is not limited by history. Hope reaches into the future and lets us enjoy all God has available for us. Through hope the impossible becomes reasonable.

Mary at the wedding feast in Cana anticipated Jesus' ministry. When they ran out of wine, she told Jesus the problem and He responded that it was not the time. But Mary was not put off; she simply turned to the servants and told them to do whatever He said to do. She had a living hope that accessed resources beyond the circumstance. Jesus responded by performing His first miracle. Mary's hope touched the compassionate love of the Savior. This willingness on the part of Jesus to trouble Himself to meet the needs of others is a key component in a revival culture.

CHAPTER SEVEN

Love: Troubling Ourselves for Others

For the love of Christ controls us...

2 Corinthians 5:14

A supernatural outpouring of the love of God marks every revival in history. The presence and power of the Holy Spirit awakens deep levels of love for God and love for others. In this atmosphere of love, obedience to demands of the gospel flows naturally from us as we share the wonderful things we see God doing. This is why a revival culture must have the unconditional, initiating love of God as its foundation. This compelling love becomes the protection against the distractions that often disrupt the fervor of revival fire and keeps us from slipping back into old patterns. Every individual needs an infusion of love strong enough to cause us to be carriers of His love to the world around us.

TROUBLE YOURSELF

When Jesus was approaching the tomb of Lazarus, Mary came out to meet him and fell weeping at his feet (John 11:32). Jesus could have ignored the emotion because, after all, within a few minutes there was going to be a resurrection. The weeping would be replaced by rejoicing. But the heart of God does not dismiss the emotions of our humanity. Jesus, we are told, *was deeply moved in spirit and was troubled.* He allows Himself to feel compassion for the friend who is in pain. Jesus was indeed touched with the feeling of our infirmities. God is not distant from the emotions we feel; in fact, He is touched even while holding in His hand a powerful deliverance from the situation.

The phrase "was troubled" here could equally be translated "troubled Himself" - in the margin of the NASB this is the alternate rendering. Think about that for a moment. Jesus is on the way to a resurrection and troubles Himself to stop and identify with the suffering of a friend. It speaks of a deliberate engagement with His ability to feel empathy for the person in need. He troubled Himself; He stopped and engaged with the feeling of the individual to the point of tears. This revelation has profoundly changed the way I conduct myself in ministry.

In the past I have imagined what it must have felt like for Jesus to be on the way to a resurrection. I knew that if I was on the way to a funeral and absolutely knew that the dead person was going to live again, I would have been on an emotional high. Bold and ready, I would have brushed past the emotion of Mary, knowing that her pain was only temporary. However, Jesus not only stopped to acknowledge the emotion, He joined in and wept with His friend. He troubled Himself to interrupt the journey to the tomb and identify with the pain and suffering. He was not so busy about the Father's business that He could not trouble Himself to take time to love deeply.

GOSPEL OF LOVE

In the Azusa Street revival the love that was poured out helped them cross the racial barriers of their day. This kind of love initiated in the heart of God and demonstrated in the life of Jesus now powers the awakening that is growing across the earth. The outpouring of the Father's love in Toronto set in motion an unprecedented expansion of the gospel. Many who were impacted have carried it around the world and several, such as Roland and Heidi Baker in Mozambique and Leif Hetland, have seen over a million respond to the gospel of love in the last twenty years. This revelation of love is more than an emotional response; it is a compelling force that puts demands on the way we live our lives. The love of God calls us to trouble ourselves and stop to share His love with others.

Nate, a revival carrier in Dayspring, was driving down the road one day and saw a man in a wheel chair crossing the street. He heard the Lord say turn around and pray for that man. His first thought was, "Oh no, Lord, I don't think I have the faith for that type of healing today." But the Holy Spirit kept insisting; so, he finally turned around and looked until he found him. The man was limping into his house from his wheelchair that he had left in the front yard. Nate pulled up to his driveway and asked him what had happened to his leg. He said that he had an ingrown toenail six months ago that became so infected that he was scheduled to have surgery in three days, and they might have to amputate his whole toe. Nate spent about ten minutes talking to him and found out that he had been in ministry when he was younger and had become offended at someone and hadn't been to church since then. Nate encouraged him in his destiny in God and then they prayed. After the prayer Nate had him stand up, and his pain had gone from excruciating down to one or two! So they prayed again and the pain was gone. A few minutes later he WALKED Nate out to his truck!

Paul describes this kind of love when he tells the Corinthians, *For the love of Christ controls us...* (2 Cor. 5:14). In this phrase Paul connects the focus and motivation of ministry with a controlling love. This is the heart of the Gospel. Everything we say and do is to be controlled by the love of God - every word, every action, and every response. The controlling influence over the method and the message is the love of God.

Control is not a word we naturally connect with love; in fact, we usually view it as a contradiction. It even feels foreign to the freedom we have found from legalism. But Paul, who taught us the "law of the spirit," describes this control as a total surrender to the demands of God's love. An all-consuming love so pure and unconditional, that it challenges all our presuppositions. A love when understood and apprehended, demands nothing less than sacrificial living in return. A love that compels us to follow Christ, submits to His Lordship, and give our lives to see the world touched by its transforming power.

God's love breaks down the resistance of our flesh and causes us to live from the Spirit. It is a kind of love that knows no barrier and stops at nothing to see the message of the gospel reach the whole earth. It is a kind of love that reaches out to others with no thought to our own welfare or well-being; this love when present will break down any barrier and cross any divide.

The Greek word *control* used here is used in several ways: to compress, to arrest, and figuratively, to compel, to perplex, to afflict, and to preoccupy.[1] It is a compound word, combining a prefix (meaning "the union which arises from the addition or accession of one thing to another"[2]) and the word "to hold together." The resulting word describes the powerful influence that results from the union of God's love with our humanity. It describes the unifying power and compelling nature of love that transcends the natural realm and beckons us to live life completely unselfishly.

This love literally "compresses" us, conforms us to the image of Christ. This love literally "arrests" us, taking us captive to Him and His purpose. This love literally "compels" us, becoming the driving force that urges us irresistibly toward His purpose. This love literally "perplexes" us, because it violates all our self-protection and calls us to live unselfishly. This love literally "afflicts" us, demanding that we die to the flesh and live to the Spirit. This love literally "preoccupies" us, filling our thoughts with His beauty and majesty.

BAPTISM OF LOVE

God's kind of love cuts across every barrier and releases His power into situations that human love could never affect. When we arrived in Africa as missionaries, I was returning to the land where I was raised, but my wife Sally was about to experience some profound culture shock. She was raised in the city and, although we had spent time in Nairobi in language school, the move to the desert in the North of Kenya was a radically new environment for her. The dry, arid terrain stirred up clouds of dust and sand every time the wind blew - a mixed blessing since the wind was needed to offset the constant 100 plus temperatures. Dirt and sand blew everywhere and into everything. It seemed no matter how well we sealed the food the sandy dust got in; but soon we became accustomed to all the food we ate having the crunch of sand.

The people we reached out to were nomadic herdsmen who moved with their cattle and camels in a constant search for water and limited grazing. Water was much too precious to use for anything other than drinking, so the idea of taking a bath was unthinkable. Instead, many would coat their bodies with red ochre that acted as a kind of deodorant, as well as insect repellant. After a while the smell seemed natural, but when first encountered, it was overpowering.

My job was fairly well defined – helping to build buildings and repair water systems. I would meet with the men early in the morning for prayer and discipleship, and then spend the day working with them to get the work done in the intense heat. Sally's role was simply to keep us alive. We bought food supplies for three months at a time, but it was necessary for everything we ate to be made from scratch. This meant hours each day spent in baking bread and making the meals as well as trying to keep up with the dust and dirty clothes.

As Sally's fluency in Swahili improved, she began to reach out to the women in the community, seeking to develop friendships. Her challenge culturally was typified in her relationship with a woman named Ingetre. Of all the Rendilli women, Ingetre seemed to smell the worst and was the one who responded most demonstratively to Sally's reaching out for friendship. Every time she saw Sally she would run up and give her a hug, leaving smudges of red ochre on Sally's clothing and the fear of a deposit of lice in her hair.

Sally fought through the struggle and continued to reach out, but the battle that raged in her was bringing her to a crisis. In the crisis she cried out to God, "We are here to love these people, but I can't do it. I am repulsed by the filth and, if You don't help me, I won't make it!" As she cried out for help, slowly things began to change. Through the Holy Spirit, God began to pour into her His love, a love that went beyond the smell and the filth. A love that gave her a new appreciation for this woman that God loved unconditionally, a love that no longer felt the repulsion of the flesh but saw into the heart of the woman and enabled Sally to make a living connection.

Over the next few years Ingetre and Sally became great friends and ministered together at every opportunity. The filth was still there but something had happened in Sally that took her beyond herself and into a dimension of love that was powerful enough to overcome her senses and connect her with a person that needed Jesus despite the cost.

The Spirit of the Initiator of love lives in us and works in us to reshape us from responders to initiators. Paul in his letter to the Romans describes this process, *and hope does not disappoint, because the love of God has been poured out within our hearts through the Holy Spirit who was given to us* (Rom. 5:5). It is a work of the Holy Spirit to put a God-like love into our hearts. The Holy Spirit who raised Christ from the dead was released onto us at Pentecost. The Spirit who breathed life into the grave is ready to breathe life into us and awaken us to a dimension of love that is foreign to our flesh. This baptism of sacrificial, unselfish love takes us out of ourselves and connects us to the heart of Jesus, the One who gave Himself unconditionally that others could be free.

RESPONDING OR INITIATING

We are not capable of producing this love in our own strength or ability. There is a built-in weakness in our fleshly nature that must be challenged and put to death. John gave us a key to help us understand it when he wrote, *We love Him because He first loved us* (1 John 4:19). At first glance it is a wonderful declaration of God's loving plan, but if we are not careful, we will miss the truth behind it. God is defining our human ability and capacity to love and showing us its limitations.

We love because... We love because God initiated love toward us. We respond to that love and love Him in return. We love because someone else did the right thing. We respond with love when someone sends the right signals or gives the right message. At our best we are hopeless responders. If someone approaches us that fits into our paradigm and wants to give us a hug, we feel the love. But if someone who doesn't smell like us and is covered in filth walks up to give us a hug, the old responder suddenly takes over, causing us to put the brakes on and offer our shoulder at best. Jesus highlighted this issue of conditional human love in His first teaching after calling His disciples, *And if you love those who love you, what credit is that to you? For even sinners love those who love them* (Luke 6:32). There is nothing unusual in loving those who respond correctly to us. But growth begins when we learn to love those who don't.

In marriage we find ourselves responding and don't seem to see the limitations of this kind of behavior. Marriage is intended to be the amazing journey of two individuals with different needs and backgrounds becoming one. But many never reach this stage, because living as a responder leaves us at the mercy of the flesh, and flesh will never give in to the needs of others. To make a marriage work there must be the injection of a love without selfish motive, a love strong enough to bridge the gap between two people and bring them together as one.

GOD'S LOVE INITIATES

John defines God's love a few verses earlier, *In this is love, not that we loved God but that He loved us and sent His son to be the propitiation for our sins* (1 John 4:10). God did not wait for us to respond to Him; He initiated love toward us without any demand that we respond correctly. His kind of love is unmoved by the response of others, because it is truly unconditional. It operates in full power. Its source is not connected to the fickle nature of flesh but to the unchangeable nature of God.

For the sake of love, Jesus the Son, at the Father's request, willingly came to earth as a man, knowing full well all that lay before Him. He dealt with the frailties of humanity as He perfectly modeled the love and compassion of His Father. He brought the rule of heaven to earth and demonstrated its power by healing the sick, raising the dead, and releasing freedom to the oppressed. On the cross He drank the full cup of the Father's wrath that paid the price for our sin. Because of love, Jesus stood between us and the punishment we deserved; His death paid the debt we could never pay. But the grave could not hold Him. He, the righteous Son, had finished His assignment and the Spirit of the Father breathed resurrection life into His beloved Son. Unconditional love always makes a way and pays the price for others to find freedom.

God initiated love toward us and we responded to that love. Our response was and is dependent on His initiation. As responders most of our actions have some component of self. Our feeble attempts at unselfishness are all tinged with motives that we hide beneath a veneer of spirituality, only to be exposed when others don't respond as we had hoped. The idea of unselfish sacrifice requires a death to self that challenges our tendency toward self-protection.

After defining this unselfish, initiating love, the writer challenges us to the unattainable. *Beloved, if God so loved us, we also ought to love one another* (1 John 4:11). How can we possibly love others in the same way

He loved us? How can we as humans learn to love one another unselfishly and sacrificially? Yet, this is more than a request; it is a commandment, we are to … *love one another just as He commanded us* (1 John 3:23).

To obey Scripture demands that we move past the limitations of being a responder and take on the divine attribute of unselfish, initiating love. It requires that we look honestly at ourselves and respond to others with the kind of grace we would like to receive. But it must be given without any demand for correct response in return.

LOVING OUR NEIGHBOR

One day Jesus was asked by one of the Pharisees to identify the greatest commandment. He gave a two-fold answer. … *You shall love the Lord your God with all your heart, and with all your soul, and with all your mind. This is the great and foremost commandment. The second is like it, You shall love your neighbor as yourself* (Matt. 22:37-39). The greatest commandment has two parts which combine scriptural injunctions found in Deuteronomy 6:5 and Leviticus 19:18. The whole law is fulfilled in a vertical and horizontal expression of love.

First, we must love God with all our heart, soul, and mind. We must love Him and be in love with Him, caught up with Him and awed by His faithfulness. Our minds are to be filled with the wonder of who He is and the goodness and grace He extends toward us. This is the first and greatest commandment, because it is the fountain out of which all other aspects of our relationship with God and others flow. If our love for God is correct, then our responses, affections and love toward others will follow in the right measure.

Second we are to, "love our neighbor as ourselves." This second half is an extension of the first. It is "like" the first, meaning that it is founded on it and flows naturally from it. This second commandment is of the same nature and of equal importance and validity as the command to love God. In fact this commandment to love our neighbor occurs eight times in scripture, making it one of the most repeated injunctions in the Bible. Many seek to grow their vertical relationship with God and pay little attention to the horizontal, their relationships with others. But, it simply isn't enough; we are commanded to do both.

We can never fully love our neighbor without first loving God and accessing His love. Conversely, we cannot claim to love God and disregard our relationships with others. Thus, loving God and loving our neighbors are interconnected. We can't do one without the other; these two are interdependent parts of the same truth. This means that our relationship with God can be measured by the quality of our relationships with those around us. The apostle John wrote, *If anyone says, 'I love God,' yet hates his brother, he is a liar. For anyone who does not love his brother, whom he has seen, cannot love God, whom he has not seen* (1 John 4:20).

The frightening part of this verse is that the fulfillment of the call of God on our lives is dependent on how well we love God and maintain love in the relationships around us. Everything God requires of us is encapsulated in these two statements. They work together to provide the framework for the whole of the Christian life. Everything Moses and the prophets spoke of and looked forward to begins with loving God and loving our neighbor. God's expressed love in Christ has the power to draw people to love God and to real love for one another. This is the measure of Christian maturity.

WHO IS OUR NEIGHBOR?

When Jesus was asked the question, *Who is my neighbor?* (Luke 10:29), He responded by telling the story of the Samaritan -- who helped a stranger in need by the roadside. In the parable the priest, the Levite and the Samaritan all saw the person in need, but only one stopped to help. It registered with all of them that there was a need, but when the Samaritan saw the man in need something happened in his heart. Jesus said that he felt compassion! What he saw caused him to feel compassion and the compassion moved him to action. Unlike sympathy that simply identifies with the pain or emotion of a situation, compassion is a powerful emotion that starts where sympathy leaves off. Compassion moves us from feeling to action. When we feel compassion there is the potential for divine intervention. A miracle is just around the corner.

LOVE IN ACTION

Compassion is the expression of God's love in us. Just look at the life of Jesus. Reading through the gospels, one cannot help but notice how many times compassion is directly connected to the release of the miraculous. Jesus felt compassion and raised the dead; He felt compassion and healed the sick; He felt compassion and cast out demons. Over and over in His time here on earth, the love of the Father was released through compassion as Jesus brought the reality of heaven to earth.

When Paul was being challenged by some of the believers in Corinth, he wrote back giving a defense of his apostleship but he also highlighted what he believed to be their fundamental problem. He wrote, *You are not restrained by us but you are restrained in your own affections* (2 Cor. 6:12). He was saying we do not hold you back; it is not the leaders' fault. They were not restricted by anything Paul or his team was doing, but they were restrained in their own affections. The word translated *affections* here is the same word translated *compassion* elsewhere. Paul was telling the church that their restraint was that they couldn't love properly. Their compassion was restrained and so the love of God that should have been expressed through them was held back, blocked and in need of a breakthrough. If they had let compassion flow, many of the issues they were facing would have simply disappeared. This is a central issue for those hungry to establish a revival culture. If we are to see sustained revival, we must deal with any blockage in our affections that keep the compassion of Christ from flowing through us.

A revival culture creates an environment in which people are compelled to love their neighbor in a practical way. They have come to understand that their neighbor is the next person they meet who needs a touch from God. They are willing to trouble themselves to show them the love of God, because they are actively looking for the opportunity to offer someone a divine encounter. Jesus ends the parable about the Samaritan with a command. Go and do like the Samaritan (Luke 10:37). God is looking for a people who are compelled by His love, who will choose to live unselfishly, carrying His powerful gospel of love to a world in desperate need of His touch.

The Samaritan man in Jesus' parable pushed past cultural norms to express love to his neighbor. His compassion crossed barriers and violated social norms. He chose to value a man that others had chosen to ignore. This new value system is the basis for the culture of honor found in any true move of the Spirit.

CHAPTER EIGHT

Honor: Heaven's Value System

...Give preference to one another in honor.

Romans 12:10

In an outpouring of the Holy Spirit, one distinguishing mark of God's presence is an awakened love for Him and for others. In this atmosphere of love, unity comes easily and honor flows naturally as byproducts of love. However, after the initial experience, if a revival culture is not in place, a time comes when the "feeling" of love begins to lift. The atmosphere appears to change and the responses of people toward one another begin to shift - now generated from the flesh rather than the Spirit. Unfortunately, the accuser of the brethren always seems to lurk in the background, looking for an opportunity to destroy the work of the Spirit. (All in the name of discernment, of course!)

Unchecked, this drift will spell the end of the move and, in fact, the history of revivals reveals that the end of many revivals has been marred with some form of dissention or division. When the enemy sees the fruit of an outpouring of the Spirit in a community of believers, he sets out to bring judgment and criticism into the mix to disrupt their harmony. This means that to sustain a move of God, a culture conducive to revival needs to be present in the church. This environment must include a new value system of honor, governing the way we respond and react. Whether their reaction comes from concern over an unusual manifestation of the Spirit or simply the way someone acts or what they wear, dishonor finds a way to disrupt the unity that sustains the move of God.

When heaven's value system takes root in a church setting, it has a broad impact. Honor serves as a key to creating diversity in the church; it allows for the proper functioning of the five-fold ministry; it is key to the development of team ministry in church leadership; it transforms marriage relationships; it provides a new paradigm for relating to children; it empowers the transfer of leadership to the next generation. In fact anywhere people interact, a culture of honor will improve the depth and quality of relationships.

The challenge as we begin to look at honor is that most teaching on honor has to do with honoring leaders. While there is an honor due those that lead, it is only one side of honor. Biblical honor is an introduction of heaven's value system into the church. It is about every individual giving and receiving honor in their relationships; it is about learning to receive people in their God-given identity. We have spent a significant amount of time dealing with issues in church life and leadership, and are convinced that most of the problems encountered would not even exist if a culture of honor had been present. So what is this new value system?

HEAVEN'S VALUE SYSTEM

Paul refers to this culture in his letter to the Romans. *Be devoted to one another in brotherly love; give preference to one another in honor* (Rom. 12:10). The word honor here means worth, value, or preciousness. It also has the idea of valuing, assessment, or appraisal. When we honor, we attribute value to an individual. But how is the value determined? If the wrong measure is used, it leads to valuing from the wrong basis. If someone serves willingly in the church and proves helpful, they receive honor. We even use honor as a means to increase our volunteer base and, because people need to feel value, they often respond to this. Conversely, if working with them is difficult, they receive little honor. Thus, as a church community we often determine the value we place on people based on their performance and, while there is some merit in this, it is not heaven's value system.

There is a Biblical honoring of people based on position. Parents are due honor, leaders are due honor, and those with governmental oversight are due honor because of their position. Our concern, however, is not about positional honor but about (learning) an honor that transcends position or performance and goes to the heart of the gospel. This means that we must choose to deem someone worthy of honor on the correct basis. One of the meanings of the word honor is "a valuing by which the price is fixed;"[1] so the question becomes what fixes the value? If it isn't their performance, then what basis do we use to set the value of the individual?

My daughter just sold her house. Before it went on the market we did a lot of work on it - painting, cleaning, repairing and then staging it to present it in the best possible light. The whole purpose was to attract buyers. But before the first perspective buyer viewed it, we had the realtor go through and set the value of the property. When she walked through, her focus was not on our hard work. She didn't even ask what we thought it was worth. Her one thought was what someone would pay for this house. Its value was set not on what we felt it was worth but on what someone was willing to pay.

The intrinsic value of a person does not, on any level, flow from how we feel about them. It does not flow from how they act or respond. It does not flow from how much they do for us or how well or badly they treat us. The value of an individual is set by one thing: how much was someone willing to pay. The answer - the price was blood!

God set the value of the individual! He determined the worth of a soul. He set the value by sending His own Son and asking Him to pay the debt we could not pay. This payment in blood sets the value of a person - not just for their salvation but also for their interactions with others. This valuation extends beyond salvation and dictates the worth of every individual we encounter. We must relate to each individual as a priceless treasure. A treasure so valuable, that the God of heaven, the God who created everything in existence with one word of His mouth, sent His Son to die for that one individual, thus setting their value as priceless.

What comes to your mind when you think of priceless? When I think of something as priceless I think of being careful. Hold in your hands a rare art object and suddenly caution measures every movement. You hold it carefully; place it down gently. In the same way when the body of

Christ sees others with their true value, it changes the way we speak, the way we act and interact. Deference comes into our speech and we exercise care not to damage someone considered so valuable by God.

A culture of honor finds root in the church when heaven's value system replaces a performance-based value. Remember, the word honor here is linked to value and more specifically to *value based on the price paid.* This is the revelation that releases honor! The value of an individual is not set by what they do or what they have done; it is set by what someone was willing to pay. So, God set the value of the individual when He paid the ultimate price, the blood of His Son. And because God sets such a high value on each individual, we must learn to treat him or her based on *His* value system. This means treating each individual with great love and care, constantly aware of their true value and worth in God's eyes.

VALUE DIVERSITY

Heaven's value system also calls for diversity. In a culture which values the homogeneous model of church growth, little thought is given to the value of diversity. Human nature always tends to gather to "those like us" whether it is about interests, gender, race or socioeconomic status. We feel more comfortable when we understand the worldview of the person sitting beside us. We feel we fit when those around us think like we think, dress like we dress and talk like we talk. However, while it may well be easier, it falls short of the glorious, diverse church that was purchased by the blood of the Lamb.

It proves much more difficult to honor across dividing lines, and yet this goes to the heart of the message of the gospel. Christ has broken down every barrier of division and has called His people to live in such a way that the gospel message can span the globe, crossing cultural barriers, unhindered by our stuff. "Remember the Titans" is one of my all-time favorite films. In a time of racial tension and school desegregation, one group broke through the barriers by a common love for football. Their success was orchestrated by friendships that crossed racial barriers and, in doing so, brought a strength that released a powerful team dynamic. Their victories proved greater than the sum of their parts because honor had replaced fear.

For He Himself is our peace, who made both groups into one, and broke down the barrier of the dividing wall (Eph. 2:14). In Christ every wall was broken down; the blood of the Son has shattered every divide and every conceivable barrier man can contrive. And He did all that so that His glorious and diverse bride could emerge. It is easy to read this as a Jew/Gentile division and so it was; but it was also more. *To the Galatians Paul wrote, There is neither Jew nor Greek, there is neither slave nor free man, there is neither male nor female; for you are all one in Christ Jesus* (Gal. 3:28). This glorious oneness crosses every divide.

LEADING WITH HONOR

If God really has given such a high value to every individual, it will have a profound effect on the way we lead. It will affect the way we speak, the way we interact, the way we bring correction. The word *preference* used in our key verse (Rom. 12:10) refers to taking leadership. The idea is to take the lead in showing honor.[2] Thus, leaders must take the responsibility of developing a culture in their community by demonstration. Honor is not about getting people to submit to leadership; honor based on God's value system means that leaders honor people by serving them and releasing them freely into their God-given destinies.

Honor absent from a church body does not indicate a church full of rebellious people. Rather, it indicates by demonstration that the leadership has created a culture lacking in honor; or perhaps more often, they have created a culture where honor comes from a faulty measure. It is easy to honor those who serve us faithfully or those who stand with us even when we encounter difficult times. However, this kind of honor is based on what a person does and not on who they are. Performance-based honor will only go so far and can never bring believers to maturity. Only an honor that flows from the intrinsic value of the individual will extend the reach of the kingdom. Only honor based on the value of the blood of Jesus Christ will be strong enough to bridge the differences in gender, race and socio-economic status and unite the church into a true body.

All we have to do is go back to Azusa Street to see that our humanity has a tendency to mess up a good thing. When the Spirit was poured out at the birth of the Pentecostal movement, it was poured into an atmosphere that challenged the norms of the day. William J. Seymour, a black preacher, led a multiracial leadership team in a time of racial segregation. The Pentecostal movement that was birthed had the opportunity to challenge the norms of society; however, some key leaders could not see past their own racism and sowed seeds of division. This lack of honor devastated the move of the Spirit and not only split the movement at Azusa but also led to a white Pentecostal denomination being formed.

The church stood with an opportunity to set the standard for kingdom life that could have broken racism in our nation much sooner. Instead, the church went with the societal norm of their day. The option that pleased the mass grieved the heart of God who paid the price of the blood of His Son in order that His body could be a glorious expression of the diversity of His nature.

To better understand the foundation for honor, we need to look at the context of Paul's use of the word. Romans chapter 12 begins with two very familiar verses, highlighting the challenge to resist the pressure of conformity to the world's view, its values and way of thinking. Resisting the tendency to conform requires that we submit to the transforming work of the Spirit. This work of the Spirit brings our minds into tune with heaven and, through a process of renewal, changes the natural patterns of thinking into spiritual thinking and understanding. This transformation enables us to know and do the will of God and see the culture of life in heaven lived out here on earth.

Honor is an operating principle of heaven and as leaders we must commit to helping grow healthy relationships in the body that cross cultural, racial and socioeconomic barriers. The love of God released into our hearts by the Holy Spirit leads naturally to honor if we will allow it. Notice that the verse that challenges to give preference with honor is followed immediately by the exhortation to not lag behind in diligence (Rom 12:10). Cultivating honor in the local church requires diligence on the part of every leader. That means it must get regular attention; it doesn't just happen! In order to create a revival culture the leadership must deliberately foster a culture of honor by placing a high value on every individual.

HONOR BEGINS WITH HUMILITY

The transformed mind that leads to a culture of honor starts with humility. ... *say to every man among you not to think more highly of himself than he ought to think; but to think so as to have sound judgment, as God has allotted to each a measure of faith* (Rom. 12:3). We are to take an honest look at our successes and failures, our strengths and weaknesses, and even look at the quality of our relationships. The mindset necessary for this honest assessment comes with an attitude of humility - not to think too highly of ourselves. Paul says there is grace for it and, do we ever need grace to deal with ourselves.

When we live in a place of humility we stay open to receive the truth about ourselves. The gentle voice of the Spirit can be heard over the noise of busyness and responsibility, only when we position ourselves to "not think more highly." The admonition here calls for a "sound judgment" or to be of sound mind. The phrase can be translated "to be in one's right mind" or "to exercise self-control." It is even rendered "to curb one's passions" in the book of Titus. The core thought is to "put a moderate estimate upon oneself, think of oneself soberly."[3]

For a new truth to penetrate, something has to change the equation. We all fall into patterns of thinking and find a place of status quo in our relationships. But if we hunger to go further, something needs to change. We won't grow by simply doing the same things, hoping for a different result; we grow by truth penetrating our defenses. We grow by taking down the walls that have divided us and by admitting that we desperately need one another. Humility provides the starting place for this kind of change.

Proverbs has a lot to say about humility and its counterpart pride. The author writes, *Before destruction the heart of man is haughty, but humility goes before honor* (Prov. 18:12). Pride carries a powerful destructive force in relationships, because pride will never let a person admit to weakness! When pride resides in hearts, the individuals can no longer receive the truth about themselves and, if we no longer hear truth, the resulting deception destroys lives and relationships. Pride in leadership has brought devastation to many in the church and brought down many in ministry. To change the dynamic of broken relationships or to simply begin to let them go deeper, humility needs to replace pride.

When humility comes, with it comes an ability to honor; but before humility we are blind to ourselves. When pride is put to death and replaced with sound assessment, we can begin to see ourselves in a correct light and acknowledge our weaknesses. We can begin to see our need for others from this new place of humility. The cloak of humility begins to hide the insecurities of self-protection and, as the old patterns of thinking are dismantled, self is no longer the focus. In a place of humility we can admit that we are incomplete and open ourselves to the possibility of deeper relationships.

HONOR TAKES FAITH

The humility Paul calls for requires faith. It takes faith to be honest, to trust ourselves to others. Faith gives us sound judgment about ourselves as well as our need for relationships. Pride hides our desperate need for others behind a mask of self-sufficiency. To begin to admit our weaknesses requires a leap of faith. And accepting that others are a part of the solution to our weaknesses takes humility. When self, powered by pride has control, any weaknesses we perceive in ourselves are viewed simply as a problem we should fix, a minor flaw in our nature that we will deal with one day. This dependence on self, hides the fact that God desires us to reach out to others. When humility meets faith, we can acknowledge that God made us with something missing so that we would always need others.

The first time I saw this in myself was related to my ability to hear and receive from my wife Sally. Several times over the first few years of marriage she would caution me that someone I was promoting in ministry had motives that were messed up. Being the typical male, I didn't listen and soon something would happen to prove that Sally had been right and I had missed it. Of course, I didn't listen any better the next time because I was working on being more discerning. I excused my lack of discernment, believing I was just more trusting (and, of course, trusting is good); therefore, even though I appeared wrong, I was actually right.

After several rounds of this cycle, I began to get the message that perhaps I wasn't listening. Sally's prophetic insight brought a good balance to me; her strength was meant to complete me. But because I didn't listen, I didn't get the benefit; my weakness wasn't being covered. I was letting my male pride keep me from receiving the completion that God had for me through my wife. The pain as I look back is how often she had to live through the consequence of my mistakes before I began to listen.

Freedom comes when we finally admit that we have weaknesses and some of those weaknesses are not something we can get over or grow out of;

rather, it is the way God made us. We are incomplete by design. We need to give ourselves the grace to have weakness but also the faith to find the relationships that will fill out those weaknesses. Acknowledgement of the weakness comes from humility. Our next step is to find the faith to ask God to give us relationships that provide the compliment for our weakness.

WE NEED EACH OTHER

One of my most enjoyable and productive relationships is with my team leader. As a leader he has tremendous strengths but, like all of us, he has blind spots. I also have strengths and blind spots. At first I found the relationship frustrating. At times he would make a statement or ask a question that I had trouble relating to or understanding what was meant. As I got to know him better I realized he had a perspective that I lacked. He saw something that I didn't see and needed to see. When this happens now I have learned to think "blind spot." He is seeing something I don't see and, if he is seeing it, I need to see through his eyes; because I am not seeing it through mine.

We each have a choice when we see things differently. In healthy relationships we don't try to fix this difference; we learn to value it. In fact, it should make us desperate to find the other parts that bring completeness. In a culture of honor we understand that no matter how gifted we are, we can never fulfill the purpose of God for our life without the missing pieces. It gives us a new value for relationships. We begin to look for others who see things differently, because we want to see what they see.

Without a revelation of our desperate need for others, we will always tend to treat relationships as expendable. If they aren't supporting or agreeing with our position, we don't feel we need them. And truthfully, we don't want to be around them; they make us uncomfortable. They make us question our position and challenge our understanding, and we all know the insecurities that kind of challenge produces! Only a revelation that we are created by God to need others who see and understand things we don't will produce in us a desperation to find and hold on to the relationships that complete us.

Too often in the body of Christ we have gathered with people who think and act just like us. This has produced a bland group of like-minded people all with the same basic strengths and weaknesses. Anyone who sees it differently is looked on with suspicion, because they challenge the norm or, even worse, they are accused of "destroying the unity." We need to cry out to God to help us move beyond this humanistic way of relating and embrace a kingdom-mindset, which allows for the amazing diversity present in God's design.

I remember when God spoke to us to move out to Oklahoma to work with the team of ministries we now relate to. We made a visit to find out more about them and to see if this would be the organic connection we longed for. After being with them for a few weeks we felt God had confirmed our call, but we had some concerns. The team was incredibly gifted apostolically and prophetically, but it was weak pastorally and evangelistically. My gifting is apostolic, but my internal motivation is as a pastor. I wasn't sure that my people-focused gifting would have room in this team. I was willing to learn from their strengths, but were they willing to learn from mine. Would this be a place where they could complete us and we could be a part of completing them, or would it be a place of frustration where we saw difficulties but had no power to provide completion?

Before we made our decision we sat down with one of the senior leaders to get the clarity we both needed. The question we asked seemed simple. If we join you, does that mean we need to be like you? The question may appear simple, but it had profound implications. We had no interest in mere conformity. We wanted to unite with a group in which we could grow together, learning from one another and together fulfill the purpose of God. We will never forget his answer; "If you weren't different, we wouldn't need you." We felt liberated!

His answer validated our gifting and made room for us. It demonstrated the recognition in the minds of the team their need for diversity. The culture of honor created by this recognition of need gives an opportunity for others to grow and develop in their gifting. The answer we received set us free from fear. It allowed us to be ourselves. Although there have been hurdles over the years, in the course of building this relationship we can say with confidence that God called us to this group of people and our destinies are connected.

GLORY AND HONOR

We often link the words *glory* and *honor* as expressions of praise and worship as we magnify Jesus. In Scripture, we are told that the Father bestowed glory and honor on Jesus and crowns Him with glory and honor. It is also clear from our discussion earlier that creating and maintaining a culture of honor has proved a key to sustaining a move of God. In fact, in the places around the country and around the world where the awakening is beginning to grow, leaders are with one voice calling the body to a place where a culture of honor replaces religious systems of judgment, criticism, and performance-based relationships.

A culture of honor is birthed in a local church when this new value system becomes normal life. When individuals begin to relate to one another based on their intrinsic value to God rather than their history, their weaknesses, or their failures. Something amazing happens when people choose to overlook faults and choose to let God's *love covers a multitude of sins* (1 Pet. 4:8). In this atmosphere of unconditional love, relationships can be restored and old wounds can be healed. As this culture of honor begins to develop, it will first challenge and change our perspective on relationships; then it creates a platform for the glory of God to be released in and through us.

Wherefore, accept one another, *just as Christ also accepted us to the glory of God* (Rom. 15:7). Accepting one another is a *glory* issue! Christ's accepting of us was to the glory of God; it was based on His unconditional love for us and expressed in laying down His life. His blood purchased our redemption and made a way for our adoption as sons and daughters of the King. The new identity He gave us was not based on our performance but on His righteousness, an identity given to us as a gift of His love. When we accept one another based on our true identity in Him, we give glory to God.

This week choose to nurture the culture of honor in your home, in your work place, and in the body. Ask God for His eyes, His ears and His heart to help you see the value of every individual. Treat anyone you interact with through heaven's value system and watch as God pours out more of His glory!!

CHAPTER NINE

Order or Life: Prioritizing for Freedom

…Where the Spirit of the Lord is there is liberty.

2 Corinthians 3:17

Several years ago I was the guest speaker in a church in Northern England. I was sharing about the grace of God and the transforming power of His love, when, right in the middle of the message, a woman on the third row let out a horrifying scream that seemed to go on forever and then turned into uncontrollable shaking and moaning. She had everyone's attention and the deacons rushed up ready to escort her to a separate room for deliverance. Even though my first thought was "demonic," I felt a check in my spirit and asked them to just let her be. When she had calmed down enough I asked her to share her testimony. She first told about the horrible lifelong abuse she had suffered and then explained what had just happened. As she heard the message, the love of God touched her heart with a profound revelation of being fully accepted into His presence. The healing power of love went to the deepest part of her being and freed her from guilt and shame and in a moment changed her identity. The sound we heard didn't sound beautiful, but it was the sound of freedom! Though it seemed out of order it was actually life.

One of the greatest challenges in revival is pastoring the life of the Spirit. Almost all revivals are marked by increased salvations, healings, restorations, transformed lives and, like it or not, unusual manifestations. When frail human flesh encounters and responds to the power of God, things can get a bit crazy. In fact in almost every revival in recorded history one can find spiritual activity or action outside of the norm. These unusual manifestations give room for those so inclined to be offended, and it makes the task of discerning between flesh and Spirit crucial.

We all agree that not everything we see in revival comes from the Spirit of God. When the Spirit touches people who are both soul and spirit, at best it is difficult to determine if a response is soul, spirit or a mixture of both. While we all believe that revival should produce maturity, immaturity will be present in any revival. This means that revival is messy business – if you want it to be neat, you will have difficulty allowing the freedom necessary to create a revival culture!

In the First Great Awakening Jonathan Edwards faced criticisms over a variety of manifestations that occurred in his meetings. In the Cane Ridge Revival, young children began to preach; this caused some to reject the movement. For the Quakers it was their jerking and shaking that led to major opposition and persecution. In the Azusa Street revival, race became the major issue; blacks and whites worshiped together and served in leadership together. Add to the mix other common historical manifestations in revivals like laughter, falling down, running, shouting, and the outcry will be, "Out of order!" Pastoring manifestations of the Spirit requires that we understand and walk the tension between life and order.

OUT OF ORDER

I remember well the visit I had to my church office several years ago after the Holy Spirit had done some incredible things during a Sunday morning meeting. One young man who was a very well respected businessman in the church got touched by the Spirit and rolled across the floor in front of the whole congregation, laughing uncontrollably for what seemed like forever. I got a visit from some of the self-appointed leaders who sat down in my office and told me that they paid my salary, therefore, they had the right to determine the subjects I could preach on. In fact they brought a list of acceptable subjects to keep things from getting out of order.

My response was, "That is easy to remedy. From today I release you from the obligation to pay us. And we will continue to serve as your pastors without taking a salary. This frees me to preach what the Holy Spirit gives me to preach." The stunned look on their faces as they filed out of the office was priceless. For the next three months we saw God do some powerful things, and we lived with supernatural provision until the same group orchestrated a "coup" and had us voted out.

Paul says that everything should be done *decently and in order* (1 Cor. 14:40). As we know, decently and in order has become the catch phrase for many complaints leveled against the work of the Holy Spirit. We often use the phrase "out of order" to mean that whatever is going on needs to be regulated or brought under control. Unfortunately, the way we use it has little to do with what Paul meant. The context for his statement was not to forbid the flow of the gifts but rather to orchestrate them so that they would flow in an orderly manner. There is a world of difference between order as direction and order as control. The Greek word *order* here specifically means to arrange in order.[2] This is much more in keeping with Webster's first definition of order, "to arrange in proper sequence," and seems to fit what Paul had in mind. His stated concern was that prophetic words be given one at a time so that they would be heard and so that there would be no confusion.

Typically, if we spend any time discussing moves of the Spirit, we will have heard the phrase *out of order* used to justify someone's dislike of something going on. We have heard it repeatedly as pastors and have used it ourselves to criticize manifestations we didn't like or perhaps, more accurately, didn't understand. Jesus came as the prophets foretold, but not as the people expected. Even John the Baptist, perhaps the most discerning man of his day, struggled because Jesus didn't meet all of his expectations (Matt. 11:2). This issue of unmet expectations is huge in times of revival. When things happen around us that are not what we anticipated, it is easy to judge them and decide they are "out of order."

Generally, we find that *out of order* has a variety of meanings. Sometimes it means, "I have not experienced this." Things we have not experienced can feel out of order, because we have no point of reference for them. Another common meaning that we frequently find is "I am not comfortable with it." Something out of my experience can make me feel uneasy or unsettled. At times there could genuinely be something wrong, but more often the Holy Spirit is challenging our presuppositions and it is making us uncomfortable.

Our religious backgrounds may define *out of order* as, "that is not the way we have always done it." We all have ways of behaving and activities we believe are normal and acceptable. These things get codified into a set of acceptable activities that make us feel secure, and as soon as something moves outside of that norm we immediately think *out of order.* Just try being the first ones to raise your hands in a traditional church and watch the looks.

Another meaning ascribed to the phrase out of order comes from fear. This meaning is reinforced when deacons visit the pastor to remind him that, "Some people won't like this," or perhaps a gentler form, "People won't understand." These two come with the implied threat that if you don't correct this, something bad will happen. Many revivals have been brought to a premature end when those with money threatened to cut off the finance if the things they wanted changed weren't dealt with.

ORDER vs. LIFE

One day Jesus stopped at a well in Samaria while His disciples went on ahead into town. While He waited, a Samaritan woman came for water. The encounter that followed was by local standards very out of order. Jesus was talking to a woman, a Samaritan woman at that, and He was alone with her. When the disciples returned they struggled with the situation. What would people think? "Jesus, we already have a PR problem, and You are not helping!" The woman was transformed by the life flowing in this supernatural encounter, but the disciples missed it because the life felt out of order. Their concern with appearances blinded them to something powerful that God was doing.

What comes first - order or life? It sounds like the chicken and egg question to me. I am pretty sure that the answer is life, not that it matters. What does matter is that we understand the priority. Life produces order that protects the life. But when the order, which protects life, becomes the focus, it restricts the new life God is releasing. By all appearances David was out of order when he brought the Ark into Jerusalem, and his wife Michal seemed to be the one following proper protocol. Yet her judgment of David left her barren and without life (2 Sam. 6:16-23). She had an order in her that did not protect life; it attacked life. Many movements of the Spirit appear a little chaotic at the onset. This apparent disorder can lead to reactionary attempts to bring order and, if it is not done with great sensitivity, easily slips into control and the movement soon ends in order but without the life.

The goal must always be life, and order must always remain subservient to life. Order does not produce life, but can maintain it by protecting the environment. So, correct order maintains life, but controlling order quenches life. The order that life needs is birthed in honor not control, because only order birthed in honor has the capacity to maintain life. *It is a fallacy to believe that if you get the order right, life will come; life is not birthed from order, life is birthed from the Spirit* (John 6:63).

In the first chapter we mentioned the second law of thermodynamics. It states that in the natural realm things tend to run down and tend to move from order to disorder. This is true unless energy is added, because "the flow of energy maintains both order and life."[2] From this it is clear that both life and order are essential.

I like the implications of the word *energy*. We understand that sometimes we get a little uneasy when someone uses a word that sounds "New Age," but we refuse to give away a word that has such a rich meaning. Our English word *energy* comes from the Greek word, meaning, "to work."[3] Paul used this word to describe *the* activity of the Holy Spirit in distributing gifts. *But one and the same Spirit works all these things...* (1 Cor. 12:11). He used it again to describe *...the power that works within us* (Eph. 3:20).

When we apply Paul's usage of the word energy, there is a direct application of the second law to revival culture. We see that both order and life come from the Holy Spirit and are maintained by the Spirit. The same Spirit that breathes life also brings order. We see this in creation when the Spirit hovered over the chaos and brought both order and life to this earth. During times of revival, one of the greatest mistakes we make as leaders is to receive life from the Holy Spirit, but then turn to our experience for the order to maintain it. To sustain a revival culture both order and life must come from the Spirit of God. The Holy Spirit will give order to the life that He brings; we just have to trust Him to do it.

Even though it appears that order and life are opposites, they are not in competition. Both are essential to revival, but they must be kept in priority. Paul warned the church, *Do not quench the Spirit; do not despise prophetic utterances. But examine everything carefully; hold fast to that which is good; abstain from every form of evil* (1 Th. 5:19-21). Both order and life are at work in this verse. Life is at work providing freedom for the prophetic to flow while order is at work examining the word for accuracy. The danger for us is that the desire to examine the word can become such a priority that we quench the Spirit. If we quench the Spirit, we suppress life and introduce control instead of freedom.

There are times when a person giving a prophetic word may need some correction. But how this is done can either maintain the flow of life or kill it. Treating people with honor means they are far more important to us than the messes they make. These kinds of discussions need to take place primarily in private; because public corrections are one of the most damaging things we can do as leaders. They communicate to everyone present: "It is not okay to try and fail in this place…"

VALUE FREEDOM

In a culture of revival one of the highest values is freedom. We must first allow freedom for the Spirit to move, and then we must give freedom for people to experience God without fear of public rebuke or correction. Paul tells the Corinthians that *The Lord is the Spirit and where the Spirit of the Lord is there is liberty* (2 Cor. 3:17). The context is that the veil has been removed and every believer is invited to come into the presence of God without restriction. The liberty of the Spirit is a liberty to break free from the restrictions of legalism under the law and discover the joy of intimacy with the Father.

The Holy Spirit, who brings life and freedom to us, also introduces a "new order." It is an order that places us under the rule of King Jesus. As we surrender ourselves to His Lordship, He invites us into fellowship and intimacy. The life that comes from this intimacy creates an atmosphere of freedom. This atmosphere is so full of grace that people feel free to try and fail, knowing that even if they make mistakes, they are loved unconditionally, and will be treated with honor and respect. Life in the kingdom comes with abundant freedom, because "where the Spirit of the Lord is there is liberty." This life of freedom is an unstoppable force compelled by love, which spreads out from the church into the community.

It feels daunting for leaders to give this kind of freedom. Consequently, we speak words that express freedom but then manage that freedom so tightly that no one really feels free. It only takes one inappropriate correction to shut someone down for years. Leadership must bear the responsibility for creating an environment where risk is encouraged, and where it is okay to try and fail. We must create an atmosphere so free, that even if someone goes too far, they feel secure because the boundaries of order are safe. God designed His church as a place of freedom without fear. As leaders we must learn that it is much easier to deal with excess than with death; Jesus' relationship with Peter is a perfect example of freedom being refined. One moment Peter wanted to call fire down, the next he tries to correct Jesus' theology, and then he reacts the night Jesus is arrested by cutting off an ear. But Peter who pushed boundaries also walked on water.

Recently, we had a visiting speaker in Dayspring who was a college professor and friend; I had not seen him in almost twenty years. As the worship began the presence of God was amazing and people began to respond. Some danced at the front, some lay on the floor, some laughed, some wept, and in the midst of it all someone gave a word of knowledge and several got healed. To me this was normal, but he was accustomed to a more typical service where we expect everyone to do what we deem appropriate in any given part of the service. By the end of the service he was profoundly changed by the liberty he had experienced. There is nothing like freedom to break the bonds of religious restriction.

LEAVEN OF DISORDER

Religion cannot tolerate freedom. Religious systems are performance-based and use order to protect position rather than to protect life. Just after Jesus fed the 4000, the Pharisees asked Him to give them a sign. Jesus answers them then turns to His disciples and gives them a warning. *…Watch out! Beware of the leaven of the Pharisees and the leaven of Herod* (Mark 8:15). It does not take much leaven to infect the whole lump of dough. Jesus warns that we must be aware of the things we allow to influence us. Order that comes from any source other than the Holy Spirit will adversely influence the culture of life in the body.

The leaven of the Pharisees is religion. When religious leaven is allowed into our leadership style, it affects everything. Instead of life and order from the Spirit, tradition and position become the foundation for decisions. And rules and punishment become the means of controlling the environment. Jesus' warning calls on us to open our minds and understand the distinction between what comes from religion and what comes from life. *But the Pharisees and experts in the law rejected God's purpose for themselves, because they had not been baptized by John* (Luke 7:30). They were experts at the law, but when life came, they were unable to recognize it. It did not fit with their religious understanding; it was uncomfortable. They missed their day of visitation because they put order before life.

There is a second leaven that Jesus warns of and that is the Leaven of Herod. Herod was the political leader of his day and represented the political system. Political systems driven by image and position are contradictory to the model of Jesus' ministry. Church politics have no place in the body of Christ because the political spirit is infected with a "divide and conquer" mindset. This leaven gives little value to people or to the truth. Both the political spirit and the religious spirit operate in fear and are powered by the fear of man. These destructive systems are out of order and must be avoided in the church.

LEAVEN OF THE KINGDOM

There is another leaven mentioned in Scripture and that is the leaven of the kingdom. Jesus says that the truth of the kingdom has an even greater power to permeate an environment than either religion or politics. At the Feast of Passover leaven was taken out of the bread, representing death of the old nature. But at the Feast of Pentecost the leaven was put back in, because the Spirit was going to be injected into us with power (Lev. 23:17). The leaven of the kingdom is the life of the Spirit. When the Spirit of God is invited into the church body, He has the power to change the nature of the entire congregation if He is given the liberty.

Jesus told His disciples to wait in Jerusalem until they were endued with power. They needed the life that came with His power in order to do what they were called to do. But for the church to receive this fresh empowerment of the Spirit, we need to allow the Holy Spirit to help us redefine order so that life becomes the priority. To be a carrier of the life of revival means laying aside disappointments, unmet expectations and the limits of past experience so that a fresh wind of the Spirit can blow through us.

Jesus told the woman at the well that, *God is spirit, and his worshipers must worship in spirit and in truth* (John 4:24). Worship brings a revelation of both Spirit and truth. Because true worship connects us to the heart of God, true worship will help us find the balance between order and life. As we learn to host the presence of God, He will help us discern the difference between order that maintains life and order that kills it. We must learn this if we are to keep from missing our day of visitation. If we stay in tune with the Spirit of God, He will show us the balance between life and order.

CHAPELTOWN

One of the most fulfilling ventures we experienced in England took place when we planted a church in an urban area of Leeds, called Chapeltown. The Chapeltown race riots of 1987 had barely died away when we moved in. Picture our family of four, plus four other young people, moving into an urban neighborhood full of drugs and violence. The local police visited us early on and wanted to rent the top floor of our home to use as a spy base, which, of course, we refused. Local drug dealers soon learned that they could hide drugs on our property because the police never searched there. When Sally discovered a stash in our backyard, she had to have a talk with one of the local dealers – we were there to express God's love, not have them arrested.

The process of building an interracial church in a cultural war zone had all the charm of a nest of hornets, but the result was amazing. The church became a living testimony to God's ability to unite His people across the races. We took our interracial worship team out onto the streets and watched as God did a wonder in that strife-torn area. The church became a testimony to the city, with a gratifying racial diversity. And even better, we genuinely liked one another.

When we arrived in Leeds we began to reach out to the other pastors in the city. We knew that the challenge of racial reconciliation we were taking on was much bigger than ourselves and we wanted and needed their cooperation. We began praying regularly with different pastors and the support we felt was extraordinary. One of the most gratifying relationships was with the pastor of a large church in the center of Leeds who had been praying for Chapeltown for years. He had made several unsuccessful attempts to get a satellite church started in the area where we lived and was excited to help us succeed. He and I began to meet regularly to pray and to strategize. His knowledge of the history and culture was invaluable.

Then the phone call came from his apostolic oversight. The short version of the content of the call would be, "Stop meeting with my leader unless you are going to join our organization." It was heart wrenching; order had just killed life! We went on with the work and God supplied others who stood with us until the breakthrough came, but something had been lost which was on the heart of God.

It was several years before the next phone call. By this time we had turned the church over to others and moved back to the States. But the next time we were in England for a visit, the pastor from Leeds called and asked if we could meet. We had a great time of restoration and he told me that his overseer had recently repented of his sectarian attitude and they wanted to make it right. To our surprise and delight they organized a joint meeting in the city in which they repented and we were restored. In that moment of repentance, life was returned to the citywide work. It is so easy to let our perception of order stand in the way of the life God desires.

When we place life before order, we give the Father pleasure and in turn He releases great joy. The joy we experienced at that meeting was tremendous, but the joy that comes as a manifestation of His presence is even greater. His joy is to become a part of our lifestyle.

CHAPTER TEN

Joy: Atmosphere of the Kingdom

With the joy of the Holy Spirit.

Romans 14:17

The first time I experienced a true joy and laughter that I knew emanated from the Holy Spirit happened in 1994. My wife and I pastored a church that was going through a very difficult time. As a result of all the turmoil, we faced the darkest and most difficult moment that we have ever experienced in our 43 years of ministry. Every morning we would spend a couple of hours at the church with those "hungry for more," just crying out to God for breakthrough. In one of those prayer meetings I had my Bible opened and was reading from 2 Kings 18 where Sennacherib prepared to invade Judah. In preparation for the invasion he was trash-talking Hezekiah and the God of Israel, hoping to demoralize the people of God.

Then I read a few verses later in 2 Kings 19:7 where God promised Hezekiah that He would arrange it so that Sennacherib would hear a rumor and turn back from attacking Judah. It struck me as ironic that someone as powerful as this tyrant would run from a rumor, and I could visualize the timidity that the Lord had put on him. I began to rejoice as I meditated on the victory of our King Jesus, then it hit me it wasn't just a rumor! Sennacherib had run from his own words! All the words he had sowed into the land had made the circuit and come back to him as a rumor! Suddenly I doubled over with laughter as I joined my Father in laughing at His enemies. For almost an hour I was out of control. I laughed till my sides hurt and still couldn't stop and didn't really want to!

And, of course, joy is contagious so, before long the whole prayer time had become "happy hour." Forgotten were the pressures and tensions we lived under as we just enjoyed the victory of our God. Inevitably, for those that wanted us out of the church the laughter proved the final straw and gave them the piece of evidence they needed. But for us it provided an amazing release into God's purpose. All fear and intimidation evaporated and a confidence filled our hearts, knowing that our Father always has the last laugh.

The joy we experienced caused great offense, as any manifestation of the Spirit seems to have the potential of doing. People appear to accept joy as theology but not as an actual experience, particularly if the experience is laughter. At the time, I heard many say that joy is an acceptable emotion for the believer in worship but not laughter. However, a quick look at the dictionary will show that as a false dichotomy. One of the definitions that Webster gives for laughter is the experience or manifestation of joy, and it goes on to say that laughter is one of the ways we express joy. Still others define laughter as an audible expression or appearance of excitement derived from an inward feeling of joy and happiness.

Religion powered by fear so often keeps us from embracing all God has available. I certainly know that it proved true for me; I had an experience but no biblical frame of reference. And all too often in charismatic and Pentecostal circles personal experience has trumped biblical truth. Aware of this from my own background, I knew I needed a biblical base for what I had experienced. As I searched out joy in scripture, I found myself meditating on Nehemiah 8:10 – *Do not be grieved, for the joy of the Lord is your strength.* It matched the experience I had; the joy and laughter had certainly strengthened me for the difficult situation we were going through. It even seemed to fit with the life of Jesus where we read, ... *who for the joy set before Him endured the cross...* (Heb. 12:2). I understood this to mean that the future joy strengthened Him for the difficult circumstances of the cross. So on one hand I had embraced the laughter but only for a limited purpose. And I had no real hunger for more and remained deeply critical of some of what I perceived as excesses.

I distinctly remember one meeting I went to in Oklahoma that I felt ended up totally "chaotic, out of order, and out of control" and left saying I would never go back. Then halfway home the Holy Spirit confronted me and asked if I was hungry for more; I immediately answered yes. Then He asked if I was willing to miss His visitation. Fairly shaken by the strength of the encounter my answer was an unequivocal, "No, I don't want to miss You!" He then said that I should not treat as common what He has made holy. I knew what He was referring to and, from that moment, I have sought never to quench the Spirit, however He chooses to manifest.

Over the next year we experienced several waves of joy and times of refreshing. We had meetings where laughter took over and others where we seemed back to "normal." There were still too many things that bothered me about the whole matter. It appeared that some of those who laughed the most and at the most inappropriate times didn't seem changed by the manifestation of the presence of God they were apparently experiencing. Yet, at the same time we saw others who were profoundly set free from life-long inhabitations. Even with all the good we saw, we were relieved when it began to lift. We looked at it as a season that had been good, but now that it had ended, I honestly was not disappointed because I still didn't fully understand it.

SEASON OR LIFESTYLE

Then several years ago we began to experience joy and laughter again. Kevin Dedmon from Bethel began ministering on living and ministering from joy! And my first thought was hang on; we have been there, done that and it is time to move on. But, as he went further in his message, I knew that the Spirit of God wanted to reintroduce a manifestation of God's presence that we had not stewarded well. As I sought God about it, He began to show me that we had treated the joy and accompanying laughter as a season but not a lifestyle. When we treat something as a season, it has a beginning and an end. If it is seasonal, we expect it to run its course. If we feel the season has ended, we don't stir it up again as it wanes. As believers we don't want anything that's not real; so, when it begins to die out we let it. The problem was that we did not understand the treasure that we had and did not learn to live a lifestyle of joy.

Look at what Jesus tells the disciples about joy, *These things I have spoken to you, that My joy may be in you, and your joy may be made full* (John 15:11). If you think of Jesus as aloof and stern, think again. Jesus' personality was marked by joy. I remember seeing the Johnny Cash movie "Gospel Road" while on our first furlough from the mission field in Kenya. The film portrayed Jesus as having fun with His disciples. In one particular scene Jesus laughed and roughhoused with His disciples and even pushed one of them into the ditch on the side of the road as they walked along. I remember saying to myself that the film looked like a more accurate portrayal of the Jesus of the Bible than most of what I was taught, growing up. He lived His life full of joy and we should do the same. His joy is in us!

As I got before the Lord I realized that I needed to repent for not valuing the gift God had given. I didn't value joy, so it didn't become a lifestyle to be worked into the lives of believers and into the DNA of our church body. God was once again offering us a chance to make it right by restoring our joy as a lifestyle, not simply an experience. He took me to 1 Chronicles 16:27 – *Splendor and majesty are before Him; Strength and joy are in His place.* God's dwelling place is full of joy! If His dwelling place in heaven is full of joy, then His temple here needs to be full of Joy! We as His temple, the dwelling place of the Spirit, surely should be marked by strength and joy. In believing for "on earth, as it is in heaven" we should expect that the same strength and joy that is in His place to be here in us. In His kingdom here on earth – power and joy should and will be marks of His rule. As individuals and as a church we choose for our lives to be marked by His power flowing through us, and His joy constantly in us.

In Galatians chapter 5, Paul lists the fruit of the Spirit. We understand that the fruit represent the character traits of Jesus, which the Spirit reveals and works into us as we live and walk by the Spirit. The Holy Spirit only reveals and works into us traits that typify the life of Christ and there in the list is joy. So joy is more than a season; it must become a lifestyle. Joy is a character trait of Jesus that He desires to be reproduced in us by the work of the Spirit. We must live our lives full of joy just like He did. In the rest of this chapter we want to lay out some of the foundational shifts that have helped us begin to create a culture of joy and see it as a lifestyle.

REPENTANCE AND JOY

Repentance has always been at the foundation of revival. Just a cursory read of revival history will give countless examples of repentance sweeping through a body of people and changing the very nature of their worship. Other revivals have become so wide spread that the repentance from sin changed the fabric of society. In the same way many of the same revivals record outbreaks of joy and laughter, but seldom were they the primary focus and did not sustain much past the end of the revival.

During this season of seeking to nurture an awakening, repentance from sin will always prove foundational. But what happens after we repent? There is another foundational truth God has established in the New Covenant that needs to be grasped by the body of Christ. Once we have repented, our guilt is gone and our joy will be restored. This is not just a suggested disposition; it must become a lifestyle of joy. After David's repentance he cries out to God, *Restore to me the joy of Thy salvation, and sustain me with a willing spirit* (Ps. 51:12). He expected that having repented, his joy could be restored. For some of us our history of Christianity has made little room for joy. The sin awareness has been so drilled into us that we almost feel guilty if we get too happy. But this time of awakening will also restore our joy.

In fact the Psalms are full of references to joy. David lived a unique relationship of intimacy and fellowship with God that was almost New Covenant. David repented for his sin and then wanted his joy back. Often our emotions are controlled by the circumstance rather than by the joy so central to our salvation. There is a time to weep, but then it is time to rejoice despite the circumstances. In fact in difficult situations it takes greater faith to rejoice in His presence than it does to weep. God's goodness, which brings repentance, also restores our freedom and joy. So, if we learn to keep our repentance up to date, we should be able to live in *continuous joy*.

Notice from David's request that the restoration of joy will be sustained with a willing spirit. Willingness proves key to sustaining the joy of our salvation. If God gives a life of joy as my portion, then any joy we show is legitimate. It is a false dichotomy to try to decide if the joy we feel is natural or spiritual. The truth is that, for a believer who has been forgiven, joy should become a way of life. If we don't feel joy, we need to be willing to violate our flesh and exercise our will to call forth joy. For those of us from deeply religious backgrounds we must willingly step outside of our history, even if it feels uncomfortable and foolish. After all, joy is an attitude of the Spirit birthed in a thankful heart – it is a choice.

We believe this truth is essential and needs to be received and implemented in our lives. In fact, this disposition of joy sustains the spirit of revival. If sustaining revival only depends on repentance, then sin is necessary to sustain revival. But if the revival stirs again the joy of salvation, it can sustain indefinitely. The presence of joy in revival should not surprise us because heaven throws a party every time a sinner repents. *I tell you that in the same way, there will be more joy in heaven over one sinner who repents, than over ninety-nine righteous persons who need no repentance* (Luke 15:7). Heaven goes crazy every time we repent! Shouldn't we choose to do what heaven does and go crazy with joy when repentance is found. Actually, joy is the only correct response to repentance.

The prophet Isaiah makes an amazing declaration about the salvation that he expected to come through the Messiah. Therefore you will joyously draw water from the springs of salvation (Isa. 12:3). He saw salvation as a spring bubbling up with a never-ending supply of healing, forgiveness, freedom and wholeness. Every time we taste the salvation that releases forgiveness, joy should flow from the well. Joy is the correct and appropriate response to salvation. This verse from Isaiah is one of the verses read during the celebration of the Jewish feast of the tabernacles.

John gives an account of Jesus' response to the Day of Atonement, the last day of the feast of tabernacles. *Now on the last day, the great day of the feast, Jesus stood and cried out, saying, 'If any man is thirsty, let him come to Me and drink. He who believes in Me, as the Scripture said, from his innermost being shall flow rivers of living water'* (John 7:37, 38). As Jesus watched the priest pour water out on the altar, He knew that, as the Messiah He would give living water to any who would come to Him and ask. Not just a single drink; it would be a drink that produced a river of living water. There is a joy experienced at this feast that is missed unless we look into the tradition of this final day of the feast. We particularly enjoy this commenter's glimpse into the atmosphere Jesus witnessed that day:

> The generally joyous character of this feast, broke out on this day into loud jubilation, particularly at the solemn moment when

the priest, as was done on every day of this festival, brought forth, in golden vessels, water from the stream of Siloah, which flowed under the temple-mountain, and solemnly poured it upon the altar. Then the words of Isa 12:3 were sung, "With joy shall ye draw water out of the wells of Salvation," and thus the symbolical reference of this act, intimated in John 7:39, was expressed.' 'So ecstatic,' says Lightfoot, 'was the joy with which this ceremony was performed-accompanied with sound of trumpets-that it used to be said, whoever had not witnessed it had never seen rejoicing at all.' Jameson Faucet Brown[1]

Catch the transition here. It begins with the solemn moment of repentance followed immediately by the most outrageous joy imaginable. Don't miss the connection; joy and laughter are released through our salvation in the same way that tears are released in repentance. The commentator goes on to say that if you haven't seen this joy, the joy of salvation, you have never experienced true, full joy. Our great salvation proves the source of indescribable joy. Pray right now, *God I want to experience this kind of joy!*

My wife Sally had her encounter with joy about the same time that I did. As we walked through some devastating circumstances, she began to pray for a revelation of the cross. A few days later we attended a small group meeting and one of the members had put some of the crucifixion scenes from the Jesus film to music. As we began to watch it, the Holy Spirit fell on Sally in a powerful and unique way. She fell to the floor weeping at the price paid for our salvation and then almost immediately began to laugh, rejoicing in the great salvation we have been offered. She was completely undone and unable to walk. The joy began to hit all of us as we watched her enjoying the presence of God. And then we lost it when the host came up the stairs with a wheelbarrow to carry her out to the car! All night long she alternately laughed and cried as the Spirit of God empowered her with the anointing and grace to face the difficulties ahead and to plant another church, Dayspring.

John the Baptist called Israel to repentance. *Therefore bring forth fruit in keeping with repentance* (Matt. 3:8). What is the fruit of repentance? Some of them appear obvious; walking in holiness and change of direction are both good answers. But we want to suggest that the power to *sustain* is connected to joy. The fruit of real repentance should lead us to a river of continuous overwhelming joy, joy so profound that it even bubbles up in laughter. We particularly like Bill Johnson's statement that puts the two revelations together, "Laughter is to salvation what tears are to repentance."

JOY AND THE HOLY SPIRIT

Let's go back and look at the very next thing John says about Jesus' declaration and invitation at the feast of tabernacles. *But this He spoke of the Spirit, whom those who believed in Him were to receive* (John 7:39). What a vital connection! The most unbelievable joy ever experienced by the Jews is directly connected to the presence of the Holy Spirit in the believer's life. The ecstatic joy of the feast of tabernacles, through the Spirit, becomes a lifetime of joy for every believer. As the Holy Spirit is poured out, the joy (present only in shadow under the Old Covenant) becomes a reality as we grasp the extent of this great salvation we have been given. To experience the Holy Spirit gives access to joy and laughter as a way of life.

In the book of Acts we read that ... *the disciples were continually filled with joy and with the Holy Spirit* (Acts 13:52). Being filled with joy comes as a result of the revelation of the Spirit, not just a manifestation of the Spirit. As Spirit-filled believers, there are times when we have so wanted the joy to be of Him that we forgot to be joyful. If you are a child of God, any joy is an expression of His life in you.

God's Word is filled with promises of joy from beginning to end. He wants us to live full of joy in every aspect of our lives, and then there will be those moments when the Holy Spirit touches the joy in us and it erupts in worship to our great King. Remember when Mary went to see Elizabeth; the baby in Elizabeth's womb leapt for joy and she was filled with the Holy Spirit (Luke 1:41, 44). Just the encounter with the presence of God was enough to release the Holy Spirit into her life and for her to know the great joy of God's promise fulfilled.

Joy is God's design! He fills us with His joy independent of our circumstances. He never gets bothered by the storm and, when our confidence is in Him, neither should we. Paul's prayer for the Romans was, *Now may the God of hope fill you with all joy and peace in believing, that you may abound in hope by the power of the Holy Spirit* (Rom. 15:13). The God of hope is ready to fill us with all joy and peace in believing. What a promise! The Spirit reveals the God of hope and our response to this great hope is out of control joy. To abound here means to overflow – the overflow of hope is joy. Others see disaster, we see hope; so up comes the joy.

One night, as several of us traveled home from a job in Arkansas, we ran into a snowstorm somewhere in the hills south of the Missouri border. Traffic slowed as trucks began to have difficulty getting up the hills and finally stopped altogether. We were stuck on a hill in the middle of nowhere. Fortunately, we had enough fuel to keep the heat on, but as the hours passed I started getting a little "antsy." About that time, Nate, one of the young men with me, said, "Isn't this the most beautiful place to be stopped?" For the first time I looked at the surroundings: moonlight glistening off the snow on the trees - in fact it was breathtakingly beautiful and I hadn't even seen it. I got so distracted by the circumstance that I had missed the glory of God's creation all around. Joy filled the vehicle as we took in the surroundings and before we knew it the hill was clear and we were on our way.

The joy we experienced that night is connected to the nature of God and not simply a manifestation of the Spirit. We were created in God's image with the capability of expressing the same emotions as our Father. When we surrender our lives and will in obedience to King Jesus, He manifests Himself in and through us. *He who has My commandments and keeps them, it is he who loves Me. And he who loves Me will be loved by My Father, and I will love him and manifest Myself to him ... and We will come to him and make Our abode with him* (John 14:21-23). The words "manifest Myself" are literal. The personality and emotions of the Father were lived out perfectly in the life of Jesus and now Jesus promises that He will manifest Himself in and through us.

One of the tasks assigned to the Holy Spirit living in us is to reveal Jesus. This is more than the transfer of factual information. The Holy Spirit is charged with working the character, personality, and even the emotions of Jesus into our lives. So the manifestation of laughter in times of great joy is more than just a manifestation of the Spirit. It is a manifestation connected to the very nature of God. Through the Holy Spirit, Jesus manifests in and through us the nature and even the emotions of our great God.

When we begin to understand that our joy is harnessed to the unfailing presence of God, it is powerful and liberating. We will not be moved by circumstance because we know the Source of true joy. And the Source is unlimited. The Psalmist said of Jesus, *Therefore God, your God, has anointed you, pouring out the oil of joy on you more than on anyone else* (Ps. 45:7 NLT). Jesus has the oil of joy and He wants to manifest His joy in us! So, our prayer becomes "Anoint us with the oil of Your joy and fill us with the wine of Your Spirit."

JOY AND THE KINGDOM

There are many reasons Jesus came to earth. But apart from speaking about His Father, the most consistent message Jesus preached involved the Kingdom of God revealed and released on the earth. The kingdom of light had invaded the earth, which had been under the domain of darkness. Jesus declared and demonstrated the kingdom as He healed the sick, cast out demons, and touched humanity with the Father's love. When we surrender to the reign of the King, His rule manifests in and through our lives in the same way it did through Jesus.

Paul described Jesus' Kingly rule in our lives to the Romans, *for the kingdom of God is not eating and drinking, but righteousness and peace and joy in the Holy Spirit* (Rom. 14:17). Our lives under the King's rule are marked first by righteousness given to us as a gift, securing our identity as a child of God. Second, it is marked by peace for the God of Peace reigns in and through us and, finally, according to Paul, one third of kingdom manifestation is joy. Joy that comes from the constant overflow of His goodness, and the joy we experience as the good news works in and through us. This is no surprise, because Jesus our Savior has been anointed with joy. The very essence of the rule of the King is joy!

God created us in His image and within that created design we have the capability of laughter. It is safe to assume that this ability came from God and that God laughs. David a man after God's heart, in seeing this, mentioned it in two passages in Psalms. Both places that speak of God laughing refer to Him laughing at the futility of His enemies. *He who sits in the heavens laughs, the Lord scoffs at them* (Ps. 2:4) and several chapters later he says, *But You, O Lord, laugh at them; You scoff at all the nations* (Ps. 59:8). When we face a difficult situation, God invites us to see the problem we are facing from His perspective. From our human vantage point it may look impossible, but from His perspective anything is possible. God looks at the opposition to His purpose and simply laughs! Then, He turns to us and invites us to do the same!

The apostle Paul tells us that we are seated in heavenly places with Christ Jesus. This being true then we should practice seeing things from His perspective. When we do, the whole situation looks and feels differently. Instead of reacting in fear or distress, we can with confidence and joy declare victory over the situation. From that place of victory we can laugh at the enemy's schemes, trusting that the victory of Jesus will begin to manifest in the circumstance we face. Let me share a testimony from a young man in the church.

John, one of the young men in our church drives an overnight truck route. One night while on the road a friend of his called and asked if he could pray for a fellow driver's granddaughter. She had been bitten by a brown recluse spider and, if it did not improve soon, the doctors were going to have to amputate her leg. When John heard this, he felt the victory of Jesus surrounding the situation and began to laugh and he could not stop. Then the Holy Spirit started to affect his friend, as well, and he began to laugh. They laughed for this girl's healing for probably 20-30 miles and could not stop. A couple of days later the friend called John at home and asked if he was sitting down. He said, "You are never going to believe this, but T-Bone's granddaughter has been healed and is going home from the hospital today!" She made a full recovery. Not only did God heal her, but He also brought joy into the presence of a family that really needed it.

Joy positions us with God. When He laughs at His enemies, we can laugh at our enemies. When we understand our right to see things from His perspective, He works on our behalf to put to flight our enemies. God manifests Himself in us and through us, and as we join Him and laugh with Him over our enemies, they have no option but to retreat.

JOY AND THE HARVEST

Across the earth we see signs of a great harvest beginning. More than one million saved in Pakistan through the healing crusades of Leif Hetland. More than a million saved in the last several years in Mozambique through Iris Ministries. Reinhart Bonnke's crusades have touched millions of lives across Africa and the list goes on. Last year while in Malaysia, I heard two Muslim Clerics on Al Jazeera television bemoaning the fact that they were losing more than 6 million African Muslims a year to Christianity. Add to this the revival culture growing in Brazil and one can easily see the signs of harvest. For the Jewish people the time of harvest was a time of great joy. John writes that, *The fields are already ripe for harvest... What a joy awaits both the planter and the harvester alike!* (John 4:35, 36 NLT).

For years we have labored to see the prophetic promise of the Father to the Son fulfilled - that the whole earth would be full of His glory. For our entire ministry Sally and I have believed to see a major outpouring of revival and we are beginning to see it. *Those who plant in tears will harvest with shouts of joy* (Ps. 126:5). The context is the amazing things God is doing. We choose to agree with David! *We were filled with laughter and we sang for joy* (Ps.126:2 NLT).

Heaven's joy is directly linked to the beauty of repentance and forgiveness. So each time we choose to forgive we step into even more joy.

CHAPTER ELEVEN

Forgiveness: Limitless Restoration

Take courage, son; your sins are forgiven.

Matthew 9:2

I still remember the visit of Corrie Ten Boom to our school in Kenya. Though I don't remember the year, I remember the impact on my life of the chapel service in which she told her story. Hearing of the secret room in her bedroom where her family hid Jews from the Nazi's stirred my imagination. Then she told about the raid on their home, the arrest of her family, and the horrors of life in the concentration camp where she and her sister were sent. She talked about the pain of watching her sister Betsie slowly die and the instruction in her sister's last words. "We must tell them that there is no pit so deep that He is not deeper still."[1] She told how she had been released through a paperwork error just before the rest of the women her age were put to death. Corrie believed that God had spared her life so that the world could know their story of God's goodness in the midst of unimaginable suffering.

Then Corrie shared a testimony of forgiveness that still impacts me today. She told us about the time she was speaking in a church in Germany not long after the war. After the service she came face to face with one of the guards from the concentration camp.

He was the first of our actual jailers that I had seen since that time. And suddenly it was all there - the roomful of mocking men, the heaps of clothing, Betsie's pain-blanched face. He came up to me as the church was emptying, beaming and bowing. "How grateful I am for your message, Fraulein," he said. "To think that, as you say, He has washed my sins away!" His hand was thrust out to shake mine. And I, who had preached so often to the people in Bloemendaal the need to forgive, kept my hand at my side. Even as the angry, vengeful thoughts boiled through me, I saw the sin of them. Jesus Christ had died for this man; was I going to ask for more? Lord Jesus, I prayed, forgive me and help me to forgive him. I tried to smile; I struggled to raise my hand. I could not. I felt nothing, not the slightest spark of warmth or charity. And so again I breathed a silent prayer. Jesus, I cannot forgive him. Give me Your forgiveness.[2]

In that moment she overcame her revulsion and reached out her hand. As her hand touched his, an incredible thing happened. She said "from my shoulder along my arm and through my hand a current seemed to pass from me to him, while into my heart sprang a love for this stranger that almost overwhelmed me." Corrie had discovered that when Jesus told us to love our enemies, He didn't leave us on our own; He gives us the love necessary to fulfill the command. And with the love, He gives supernatural forgiveness, which frees us and allows us to fully release the other person.

Even though it has been years, I can still feel the impact of her story. It was the first time I heard anyone speak about experiencing God in such a practical way and it changed my view of the power of forgiveness.

JESUS' PRAYER

Her experience also gave me a new appreciation for what Jesus did on the cross. In His final moments of suffering He entreated the Father to forgive those who were putting Him to death. They did nothing to deserve it, but forgiveness is in His nature. This kind of forgiveness was demonstrated often as He connected forgiveness with the miracles He performed. The paralytic in the Temple was forgiven before he was healed as Jesus demonstrated both His power to heal and the authority to forgive. The woman caught in the act of adultery was forgiven. Forgiving others must become a natural part of our life as we follow Jesus.

Forgiveness was a theme when Jesus taught His disciples to pray, *Forgive us our sins as we forgive those who have sinned against us* (Matt. 6:12 NLT). From childhood we are taught to ask forgiveness for our sin, and John tells us that, *if we confess our sins, God will forgive us* (1 John 1:9). But the second half of Matthew 6:12, *as we forgive those who sin against us* has always been more of a challenge. It is amazing how difficult it is for us to grasp our responsibility.

After over forty years in pastoral ministry, we have come to see forgiveness as the central issue in maintaining unity of the Spirit. In every situation where we have seen relationships implode and the Holy Spirit quenched, unforgiveness is somewhere in the mix. In revival history, the failure to sustain has often been the breakdown of relationships, with unwillingness to forgive as the cause. To sustain revival we need a fresh revelation of forgiveness to take root in the church. This means forgiveness is a core value for a revival culture.

Before we go further, look at some definitions. Webster says that to forgive is to stop feeling anger toward the person or situation, to stop blaming the person or situation and to stop requiring payment of what is owed. He goes on to say that to forgive is to give up any feeling of resentment. The word pardon is a synonym, which means to refrain from imposing punishment on an offender or demanding satisfaction for an offense. Finally, Webster says that to *forgive* is to grant pardon without harboring resentment.

PETER'S QUESTION

One day when Jesus was teaching, Peter made personal application of all he heard. He went to Jesus and asked, *Lord, how often shall my brother sin against me and I forgive him, up to seven times?* (Matt. 18:21). On the surface this sounds good and seems noble. In fact, Peter probably had put a lot of thought into it; seven is the number of perfection or completeness. It is the number of times blood is sprinkled on the altar in Leviticus. Peter probably also knew that the Rabbis taught that they must forgive three times before it was alright to retaliate. He knew Jesus would give more grace than the Rabbis. So seven felt right!

Peter had begun to grasp the significance of forgiveness, but his understanding still seemed to be based on some wrong beliefs – some of the same suppositions we tend to make when faced with situations in which forgiveness doesn't come easily. We see three assumptions behind Peter's question that can profoundly affect a person's willingness to extend forgiveness.

First, he is assuming that forgiveness was connected to the response of the other person. By asking the question, he was assuming that at some point, if they don't respond correctly, we have a right to withhold our forgiveness. He is implying that forgiveness can wait until the other person changes. Second, he believed that there was a limit to how often we should forgive. In giving the number seven times, he sought to be generous but in reality had set a limit on forgiveness. Finally, he assumed that he had a right to withhold forgiveness without consequences or, at the very least, he saw it as his choice to decide when and how much he needed to forgive. So, let us look at these subtle distortions, one at a time.

CAN FORGIVENESS WAIT?

We want the person that has hurt us to change in order for it to be easier for us to forgive. If someone who has wronged us comes to us with a repentant heart, we find it easy to forgive. If they don't, it gets more difficult. The truth is that many times we don't get the satisfaction of seeing the other person change. When the person remains the same, the demand for justice kicks in, and we withhold forgiveness because we want to see them pay the price for what they did. Many get stuck here, waiting for someone else to do something. In doing so, we become the victim - their mistake binds us in unforgiveness.

To break free from this trap we must understand that withholding our forgiveness goes against the heart of the gospel. God initiated forgiveness toward us by sending His Son before we responded to Him. Jesus forgave the crowd that had Him crucified before they repented and He asks that we do the same. There is a cost to forgiveness!

The basic meaning of the Greek word *forgive* is "to send away." The idea is that when we forgive we let something go from ourselves. When we forgive someone, we set them free; we release them and hold no power over them. The English word *forgive* carries a similar meaning. It is a compound word made up of the prefix "for" which means before or in advance and "give." So to forgive is to "give in advance." This means that we are to give them forgiveness whether they have "earned" it or not. At the same time, when we forgive we are giving up any resentment, bitterness or anger against the person or people involved. We are also giving up our right to demand restitution.

If forgiveness means to give in advance, then we must learn to forgive before getting a correct response from the other person. We must forgive without making change in them a condition of forgiveness. We must forgive in advance of getting an apology from them. Actually, we are to forgive them no matter what they do.

My relationship with my father was troubled at best. His attitude and anger set a poor example of fathering. Over the years his reactions built a deep resentment and anger in me. Several times I remember making the statement that I would never be like him, and I set myself to be different, more like some of the other fathers I saw as I grew up. I seemed to be succeeding until Sally and I got married. When we first had children my behavior began to change. Sally saw it and warned me that I was becoming like my father, but I didn't want to believe it.

Things came to a head when we took over the pastorate of a church in Ripon, North Yorkshire. My reactions toward our kids, particularly my son Philip, began to deteriorate. One evening I backhanded him; he lost his balance and fell, cutting his head. It finally got through that I needed help, and I drove several hours to a visit a friend I knew that ministered in inner healing. It didn't take very long for him to uncover the inner vow I had made "to never be like my father" and he showed me how bitterness had held me captive all my life. As we prayed he helped me break the vow and forgive my father. For the first time in my life I was free and from that day the power of the anger that had controlled me was gone.

My freedom came independent of any change on my father's part. Until the day he died, he never acknowledged or repented for his actions. But his lack of repentance had no bearing on my freedom. I forgave him, let him go, held nothing to his account, and required nothing from him. I wish the story had a marvelous restoration, but it didn't. I would love to have been reconciled to him, but his hurt never allowed him to open the door. If forgiveness was in any way dependent on the response of my father, I would never have been able to be free; but it wasn't. Forgiveness had the power to free me, with no reciprocal response from him.

DOES FORGIVENESS HAVE A LIMIT?

Now let us consider the second assumption in Peter's question. Is there a limit to forgiveness? This seems really logical we think, "I don't want to make it too easy on them." It seems like there should be a limit. After all, if they keep doing the same thing, we should be allowed to withhold forgiveness to make them accountable for their actions.

Look at Jesus' response to Peter's question. *Jesus said to him, 'I do not say to you, up to seven times, but up to seventy times seven'* (Matt. 18:22). I don't think Jesus was saying we should forgive 490 times and then stop. I think His number could be a reference to the lifespan - seventy years times seven for perfection. It could even be a reference to the seventy and sevenfold vengeance against Lamech (Gen. 4:24), showing that forgiveness should always exceed vengeance. Whatever the specific meaning, the idea is that there should be an unlimited flow of forgiveness.

Peter's question comes after Jesus had taught the disciples to pray and there is a truth about the limitless nature of forgiveness that Peter had missed. They were taught that there is a direct relationship between giving and receiving forgiveness (Matt. 6:12). The amount of forgiveness they wanted to receive was released by the amount of forgiveness they were willing to give. Our receiving forgiveness is directly tied to our willingness to give forgiveness.

The next verse makes it clear, *For if you forgive men for their transgressions, your heavenly Father will also forgive you* (Matt. 6:14). This is an "if/then" statement. If we forgive, then we are forgiven. The only action demanded for us to receive forgiveness is to forgive. There is no limit to the forgiveness from Christ, just as He is asking us to have no limit in our forgiveness. The limitless nature of forgiveness has its source in the blood of Jesus. He died once for all (Heb. 10:10). With one sacrifice, He secured forgiveness for all time. The sacrifice is limitless; therefore, the forgiveness it purchased must also be limitless.

The only limit is a self-imposed one. *But if you do not forgive men, then your Father will not forgive your transgressions* (Matt. 6:15). The only limit on forgiveness is in refusing to forgive. There are times when we feel that it is some sinful act that blocks us from receiving forgiveness; when actually, it is our own unforgiveness.

The story of Joseph (Gen. 37-50) is an example of unlimited forgiveness. He was one of the younger sons of Jacob and apparently the favorite (a problem for his brothers). Early in his life God gave him visions of his future, which he talked about constantly. His brothers got so sick of hearing about his dreams that they decided to sell him into slavery; then they told their father he had been killed. Over the years the brothers probably thought Joseph was dead, but God had raised him to a powerful position in Egypt.

During the famine when the brothers went in search of food, they came face to face with their sin. Joseph had the power for retribution but chose forgiveness. He ended up caring for the whole family in Egypt throughout the famine. But when their father died, the brothers panicked, because they were afraid that Joseph would take his revenge (Gen. 50:15). They did not understand the depth and magnitude of the forgiveness that Joseph had extended. Joseph was broken-hearted that his forgiveness had not been fully received. He called the brothers together and told them that he refused to play God. He had no choice but to forgive and stay in the place of forgiveness, because he was standing in his destiny as a result.

In 1990, Nelson Mandela had just been released after twenty years in a South African prison. Many feared retribution, but he immediately began a process of reconciliation between the races in his nation. At one of the rallies he made a profound statement on forgiveness. "We especially need to forgive each other, because when you intend to forgive, you heal part of the pain, but when you forgive, you heal completely."[3]

THE CONSEQUENCES OF UNFORGIVENESS

The third implication in Peter's question is that at some point forgiveness becomes optional, meaning that there are no consequences to unforgiveness. Jesus answers this in the very next parable, a continuation of His answer to Peter's question (Matt. 18:23-35). He told the story of a king who wanted to collect on the debts that his workers had accumulated. One owed him an enormous amount of money. When the worker begged for mercy, the master felt compassion and forgave the debt. The servant who was forgiven then found a fellow servant who owed him a much smaller amount of money. When he couldn't pay, he had his fellow worker thrown into prison. The king found out and was furious and he withdrew his pardon. He told him "You should have had mercy on your fellow slave, as I had mercy on you."

Then Jesus delivered the verdict on the assumption that to forgive is optional. *So shall My heavenly Father also do to you, if each of you does not forgive his brother from your heart* (Matt. 18:35). Ouch; not only do we have to say the words, they must come from the heart.

FORGIVE FROM THE HEART

So what does it mean to forgive from the heart? Look back in the story we just read at the response of the king as he forgave his servant. *And the lord of that slave felt compassion and released him and forgave him the debt* (Matt. 18:27). I find three distinct things in the response of the king to describe the nature of God's forgiveness - the kind of forgiveness he is looking for in us when He asks us to forgive from the heart.

First, he felt compassion. Compassion is God's love in action in and through us. Compassion is to be deeply touched by the love of God, causing us to respond like He would respond. Compassion allows us to release mercy, which releases forgiveness. Forgiveness from the heart is an extension of the love of God flowing through us as compassion toward the person who hurt us. In counseling, one of the ways we know whether the person has truly forgiven is by how they feel toward the other person. If they have no compassion, the forgiveness is not yet from the heart.

The second thing the king did was to "release him." If I forgive and then demand a correct response from the other person, I have not understood forgiveness. John records Jesus statement that, *If you forgive the sins of any, their sins have been forgiven them; if you retain the sins of any, they have been retained* (John 20:23). When we don't forgive, there is a hold we have over them. The word retained means to have power, be powerful; to be chief, be master of, to rule: to get possession of, to hold. When someone owes us, we are in a position of power. Literally, we hold something over them. So when we forgive from the heart, we release all the emotion we have been holding due to the unforgiveness and set them free. As we release them, the bondage of unforgiveness is broken and we are set free, as well.

The final thing the king did was to forgive the debt. Debt can be monetary; but more often it is our need for justice. In being wronged, our desire is for vindication and it is difficult for us just to let it go. Forgiveness from the heart is being willing to clean the slate and walk away. When we forgive from the heart, it frees us to step into the blessings of God's provision.

One of my friends got into some serious financial trouble several years ago, causing many to lose a substantial amount of money. Several of those from whom he borrowed have struggled to forgive him and years later are still bound by it. Others chose to forgive and treated the debt as a gift to the Lord. Almost everyone who responded in that way has seen a turnaround in their finances and is living under the blessing of their forgiveness.

Scripture ties forgiveness and money together directly. Mark writes, *And whenever you stand praying, forgive, if you have anything against anyone; so that your Father also who is in heaven may forgive you your transgressions* (Mark 11:25). The fruitfulness of our offering is affected by unforgiveness. If we are not right with one another, we rob the life from our gift. But if we will forgive, then the blessing attached to the gift will be released.

THE FATHER'S HEART

Luke records the parable that we refer to as the "prodigal son." In truth, I think it is more about the forgiveness of the father. What the son did in taking his inheritance early was a shame to the father and by law he could have disowned the son and even killed him. But the father was not inclined to condemnation but to redemption. Every day he looked down the road waiting for the son to return. Finally, the son came home hoping for a position as a servant. Instead, he was treated as an honored son. This level of forgiveness is absolutely stunning. God can forgive in a moment and combine it with full restoration of benefits.

Katie came from an abusive family life. Her father left before she was born and she never bonded to her mother. Her sister took care of her for the first 3 years of her life. For years Katie was severely abused by both her mother and brother. At 16 her life took a turn for the better. She was kicked out of the house and a high school teacher took her in. She struggled through life with a lot of pain, rage, fear, and a deep ache of emptiness. Katie is now 35 and, in the last several years, God has done an amazing work in her life through forgiveness. God has given her the grace to forgive and release her mother. Katie had a deep father wound caused by abandonment. When she forgave and released him, she was finally able to connect to Father God in a way that she had never known. The ache of loneliness and emptiness vanished as she was filled with the love of Father God, her Daddy. She now knows that she is absolutely complete in Him! She is no longer an orphan. She is His daughter.

How complete is His forgiveness? The most striking example of this in scripture is that God allowed Jesus, His perfect, sinless Son, to be born through the lineage of David and Bathsheba. To be born through the lineage of David is the fulfillment of prophetic promise, but to be born though David's union with Bathsheba is an act of forgiveness and restoration almost beyond our finite comprehension. A God who is that willing to forgive and restore requires that we learn and live in this same level of forgiveness and restoration. Forgiveness as a lifestyle will break down barriers of division and lead us into unity with each other.

CHAPTER TWELVE

Unity: That the World May Know

That they may be perfected in unity, so that the world may know...

John 17:23

Most moves of the Spirit in history have an uncommon sense of unity. This relational unity helps maintain the fire and serves as one of the recognizable marks of revival. As we consider the lifecycle of various moves of God, it is easy to see the part unity played. Even if it wasn't obvious leading up to the outpouring, as soon as the fire of revival began to burn, unity played a major role in sustaining the presence and power of the Holy Spirit. Relationships were restored and people were reconciled to one another. Tragically, however, the end of a revival has historically been marked by the disruption of the very unity of relationships that had once sustained it.

We must then recognize that maintaining healthy relationships is a primary key to hosting the presence of God. We have all been around Church long enough to know that unity can be illusive and at times seem out of reach. However, if unity is essential for the world to know Jesus, then it must become a priority in our thinking. To sustain a culture of revival requires that we understand the purpose and nature of Biblical unity in order that we both value it and guard it in the body of Christ.

Jesus' prayer, recorded in John, has a lot to say about the nature and source of unity, as well as its function in releasing the power of God into the world. But it also gives a glimpse into the relationships Jesus maintained in His life. *I in them, and Thou in Me, that they may be perfected in unity, that the world may know...* (John 17:23). Notice the three relational components of His prayer. Jesus maintained His relationship with the Father, His relationship with those He worked with, and His relationship to His mission. He then prayed that we would learn to do the same.

The first and primary relationship is to the King: *I in them.* This relationship is the mystery of the ages - "Christ in you the hope of glory" - the King living in His subjects. It is a mystery, but the revelation that we are in Him and He is in us provides the foundation for our passion and forms the basis for our intimacy with Him. This passion becomes the controlling passion of our lives so that we no longer live for ourselves, but we live for the King.

The second relationship is with the Body of Christ: *...that they may be perfected in unity....* Our passion for God must have a horizontal outworking in our relationship to the body. The link between our passion for God and the world being touched is the strength of our relationship with the body of Christ. Without unity in the body, the world will only see a distorted Jesus. It is impossible to function fully in our spiritual calling without getting our relationships healed and in order.

The third relationship outlined in this verse gives our mission: *...that the world may know....* True unity will always have purpose. Our purpose is NOT unity. Our purpose is that the world would see Christ revealed through the unity. Our mission is to 'Make Jesus King' by becoming a true reflection of His glorious nature. Our commission is to make disciples of all nations, teaching them to relate correctly to God, to relate correctly to one another and, finally, to impact the world they live in with the message of Jesus.

His presence in us is given to us to produce a unity that will impact the world. The way we respond to one another is one of the best glimpses of the love of God people will ever see. Unity in the body of Christ provides a visible expression of God's love at work; but to uphold this all three of these relational commitments must be maintained and kept in balance.

PERFECTED UNITY

The world has not seen the kind of unity that Jesus prayed for. They have not seen us love one another unconditionally. And because they have not seen us love in this way, they have no idea how much God loves them. It is time for change; it is time for the church to demonstrate the God-breathed unity He paid for. This oneness creates an atmosphere of love and acceptance so attractive that it draws people to Jesus.

The goal of our relationship with Christ and the presence of His glory is to produce Godhead-like unity that will impact the world. *And the glory which Thou hast given Me I have given to them; that they may be one, just as We are one* (John 17:22). The Godhead exists as three different persons with different roles, responsibilities, and characteristics - yet completely one. One of the best illustrations of this is water, which exists as liquid, solid, and gas – water, ice, and steam – three manifestations of the same element but one in substance.

Notice the basis for unity that Jesus outlines: He describes unity as oneness that flows from the Trinity to us through our union with Christ. *…that they may all be one; even as Thou, Father, art in Me, and I in Thee, that they also may be in Us; that the world may believe that Thou didst send Me* (John17:21).

This perfect unity can only be found in absolute surrender to the indwelling presence of the Holy Spirit - a surrender that mirrors the relationship between Jesus and His Father and enables us to represent Them to the world. Heaven's unity is not based on fellowshipping around the lowest common denominator. It is found when we make the commitment to represent Jesus' nature unconditionally and then diligently manifest heaven's value system of acceptance, honor and unconditional love.

It is clear again from this verse (John17:21) that Christ in us is to produce a unity that will impact the world. This makes the pursuit of unity far more than simply maintaining an environment of peace; it is crucial to the revelation of who Christ is and to the revelation of His glory.

We ask for His Glory, but perhaps we have not understood that glory looks a lot like unity. The more Glory the more unity. As we see revival break out, it is going to release even more unity. One of the significant historical manifestations of God's glory in the United States was during the Cane Ridge Revival. There were times when as many as seven preachers from different denominations were preaching at the same time in a huge open field, some standing on logs, others preaching from the back of wagons (all experiencing similar results). There were all kinds of manifestations of the Spirit, and it is estimated that as many as 25,000 came out of the back woods to the open field to experience what God was doing.

The unity flowing from the life of the Spirit saw more than 10,000 added to the Methodist, Presbyterian, and Baptist churches during this period. Barton Stone, one of the key figures during the latter part of this revival, has on his gravestone his life motto: "Let Christian unity be our polar star."[1] This may not be the way we would state it, but to live in revival, unity must be seen as an attainable goal.

ACCEPTANCE

So, how do we get there? Unity begins with acceptance! Paul tells the Roman church that they were to ... *accept one another, just as Christ also accepted us to the glory of God* (Rom. 15:7). Accepting one another is a glory issue. Just as Christ's accepting of us was to the glory of God, our acceptance and honor of one another is to the glory of God.

Acceptance is more than just trying to get along. The Greek word Paul used in this verse means 'to take' or more specifically 'to take in addition.' Acceptance means to make room for another person and add them into our relationships. Literally, biblical acceptance means to take them by the hand and make them a companion, to become a friend who brings the one we accept into our home and gives them access into our heart.

Although the Reformation served as a turning point in church history, bringing salvation back to grace and faith alone, it inadvertently also spiritualized the art of division over doctrine. None of the reformers initially wanted to leave their institutions; they wanted to reform them from the inside. They understood the unity of the body and wanted to protect it. However, the rejection of their message forced them to leave and start new denominations. The unintended consequence of this has been that division in the body of Christ has become acceptable. No longer are we fighting to stay together; we assume that our differences should automatically drive us apart. We didn't get this understanding from the Word but from our experiences. We believe that as the awakening grows, this trend is going to be reversed and we will see the value and power of Spirit-breathed unity in the Church.

Jesus taught us to pray that the will of God would be done on earth as it is in heaven. The will of God in sending Jesus was to extend to every human being the opportunity for restored relationship. God accepted us when we were in desperate shape, completely unworthy of His gift of grace. Now, He asks us, here in this time and place, to be as accepting and forgiving as He was. Each time we extend His love and acceptance to others, His *glory* grows brighter. As this truth takes root in the Church it will produce a multigenerational, multicultural, and multiracial unity that invites and releases the *glory* of God in ever-increasing measure.

True revival culture fosters a Spirit-breathed acceptance in our dealing with others, particularly, when there are differences in our perspective or understanding. While acceptance serves as a primary ingredient in the unity Jesus wants for His church, it doesn't just happen; it takes work. Paul makes this clear to the Ephesians when he tells them that they must focus on, ... *being diligent to preserve the unity of the Spirit in the bond of peace* (Eph. 4:3). Unity is to be preserved. The bond of unity, especially in its infancy, is fragile; it only takes a careless word or a foolish action to cause people to pull away from each other. The Greek word *preserve* means: to attend carefully, to keep in view and to apply one's self. It also means to guard from loss or injury or to prevent from escaping.

The idea here is that whenever or wherever you see unity, focus on preserving it. The effort required to do this is directly proportional to the value we place on the unity we see. If we don't place a high value on unity, we will have little hope of preserving it. Maintaining unity requires a real effort on our part.

We repeat: unity doesn't just happen. Though it is a work of the Holy Spirit, it requires something from us. Diligence! This Greek word *diligence* means: to make haste or to hurry.[2] The idea is that in order to remain united, there is no time for delay; issues need to be dealt with immediately; otherwise, the opportunity for resolve can be lost. Diligence also means: to treat it seriously or respectfully, to become proficient, or to put in work, effort or zeal.

From the definition we see that we must make unity a priority. We need to treat it seriously to the point that we become proficient. This requires a new mindset and a refocusing of priorities. We can't assume that unity in the body will be protected; it takes effort. We must learn to treat people with respect and dignity even when we disagree. If we stay alert and treat our relationships as important, then the body remains unified. This can be done as we dedicate ourselves to preserving unity by keeping short accounts and by being constantly ready to forgive and extend grace.

The second phrase in this verse is ...*the unity of the Spirit*. Unity is not found when we can come to agreement on every point of doctrine but in common sharing of the life of the Holy Spirit. When the Holy Spirit fills the believer, His task is to reveal Jesus. A vital part of that revelation is the unity of the Godhead - the perfect oneness that flows between Father, Son, and Spirit. So, the more the Holy Spirit reveals Jesus, the more unity should become normal in our Christian experience. When the Holy Spirit is present, we become more attached to our identity in Christ than to our broken history. For years before the Azusa Street revival, William J. Seymour had believed that when the Spirit fell, He would break the power of racism and prejudice. This proved such a central part of his understanding that when the Spirit was poured out, he led the revival with a multiracial team in a time of segregation. One newspaper reporter commented that, "The color line has been washed away in the blood."[3]

The third phrase is ...*the bond of peace*. Spirit-breathed unity requires a bond that holds us together. The Greek word *bond* is used for the ligament that holds a joint together. Without ligaments, the physical body would be painfully dysfunctional. Can you imagine reaching out to do a task and your hand falls off? If you saw a foot lying on the sidewalk, you wouldn't think how good it looked. No, immediately you would think someone is missing a foot. So it is with the body of Christ. God's intention is that we are held together by relationships of sufficient strength that the will of God can be accomplished here on earth as it is in heaven.

SPIRITUAL MATURITY

To further define the kind of unity Jesus is referring to let's look at the Greek words used in John 17:23. The phrase *perfect unity* essentially means to be "made perfect in one;" however, it is not a passive oneness. The word also conveys the idea of carrying through to completion, to accomplish, or to finish the process. Unity is position, but it is primarily a *process in pursuit of a goal.* Paul refers to this process when he speaks of Christ being formed in us. One translation of this passage reads, *Oh, my dear children! I feel as if I'm going through labor pains for you again, and they will continue until Christ is fully developed in your lives* (Gal. 4:19 NLT). So, being in perfect unity requires that each of us move toward completeness by adding into our lives all that is lacking. It means that we each deliberately allow the Holy Spirit to help us reach the full measure of Christ-likeness.

The fullness of Christ proposed in scripture is a required end if the world is to be touched by the glory of God. However, it is not just an individual goal; it is a corporate goal. I can't find unity in isolation. When Paul says that he labors until Christ is formed in us, he understands that Christ formed in us individually will perfect us corporately into unity. Christ in us causes us to be formed into an expression of His body: a complete body that represents Him in the earth, a body so united that the world gets a glimpse of His glory and is impacted by His power.

The phrase *perfect unity* also carries the idea of bringing to maturity;[4] the implication of this is that Christian maturity is never simply an individual pursuit. In fact spiritual maturity is an unattainable goal outside of the corporate body. Maturity develops in individuals when individual believers surrender themselves to the demands of relationship to the corporate body. In the body, growth comes as the believer interacts with others who look, think, and act differently. We can only learn to love as God loves when we are put to the test through interactions with others and choose to respond correctly. This God-ordained interdependence within the body produces both maturity and unity.

Being vitally connected to others is essential to our spiritual development. Not only is unity in the body necessary for outreach by giving a living example of the love of God, but it also proves vital to the process of spiritual maturity. It is the creative tension of living surrounded by diverse personalities, perspectives and gifts that produces true Christ-likeness in us. With this knowledge, we can joyfully embrace the maturing process, which ends in the perfected unity of the body.

Paul makes this connection between unity and maturity when he writes to the Ephesians: *...until we all attain to the unity of the faith, and* *of the knowledge of the Son of God, to a mature man, to the measure of the stature which belongs to the fullness of Christ* (Eph. 4:13). In Paul's mind unity and maturity are closely linked. The standard of Christ-likeness requires perfected unity. Faith and knowledge of Jesus, in and of itself, will help our growth but in isolation will fail to bring us to maturity. Christ-likeness requires that faith and knowledge of Jesus draw us together in unity; only then from that place of unity will we measure up to the full standard of Christ.

The Greek word "*attain*" is defined as: to arrive at, to reach a goal.[5] We have not as yet reached it; but we can and must pursue it until we do. We must see unity as an attainable goal; it is the prayer of Jesus. So our expectation should be that the closer we get to Him, the more unity will become a reality. Maturity is described here in a context of unity. Maturity that moves us toward the fullness of Christ should also bring us to unity.

One of the best examples in Church history of a sustained revival is the story of the Moravians and the 100-year prayer meeting birthed out of revival. It is also a graphic illustration of the perfected unity Jesus prayed for. As you read this brief account, let faith rise for God to do this in your life, your church, and your city.

THE MORAVIAN PENTECOST

Count Zinzendorf was a rare example of a man of wealth and prestige who was fully sold out to Christ and His service. Born in 1700 he grew up in a Lutheran family and received Christ at a young age. Then at nineteen years of age he had an encounter, which would change the direction of his life. While traveling in Europe he read an inscription on a painting in an art museum – "All this I have done for you; what have you done for Me?" This so convicted him that he dedicated his life to Jesus. He wrote his family that "I firmly resolve to live for Him alone who laid down His life for me." The passion of his life became Jesus and he spoke often of His blessed presence. Zinzendorf grasped the centrality of the suffering and death of the Savior and would later in his life come to understand the unity of all Christians in Christ and the work of the Holy Spirit in mission. This man, who church history has dubbed the rich young ruler, became a radical follower of Jesus Christ.

In 1722, the year the Count married, he received a request to help religious refugees from Moravia and Bohemia. He agreed to give them sanctuary on his estate in Saxony because he had a vision to establish a model Christian community that he called Herrnhut (the Lord's watch). Initially, he only laid down two criteria for joining the community. First, they must be "compelled by persecution" and, secondly, that in all their meetings they remain loyal to the Augsburg Confession, the primary tenants of Lutheran faith. Some of the first refugees offered asylum were Lutheran Pietists with their emphasis on personal piety over religious formality and orthodoxy. They were soon joined by Bohemian Brethren, an underground remnant of followers of John Huss who suffered centuries of persecution. Their unity of the brethren teaching allowed them to readily accept the guidelines as they found a secure new home.

Over the next five years the community at Herrnhut grew to 300 as more sought refuge. The first settlers who had all held a common theology were joined by believers from other backgrounds. Those from a Reformed persuasion came with their Calvinist theology. Others were Separatists, who felt renewal could only come outside of any organized religion. Some were Anabaptists who came wanting to introduce their form of baptism and there were even a few Roman Catholics thrown into the mix. As the diversity of the community increased so did the growing pains. Divisions over baptism, predestination and holiness created warring factions who were deeply divided and critical of one another. By early 1727, theological tensions literally threatened to destroy the community. Hutton writes: "As the settlers learned to know each other more, they learned to love each other less."[6]

Zinzendorf's vision for a model community appeared ready to self-destruct. In the early days he had little involvement with the life of the community and left management to others. As long as the settlers stayed loyal to the original guidelines, he gave them wide latitude in their practice, including the introduction of some of the Brethren hymns in their meetings. But as tensions grew the Count realized it was time to be more proactive. Feelings were running deep as Hutton writes, "the time had come to take stern measures. He had taken them in out of charity; he had invited them to the meetings in his house; and now they had turned the place into a nest of scheming dissenters."

Zinzendorf left the Dresden court and moved to Herrnhut to devote full time to pastoring his beloved community. He began by visiting each member of the community pleading for unity, love and repentance. Through a combination of Spiritual authority and charismatic personality, he called on them to focus on the areas of agreement and not their differences of doctrine. Then in a corporate meeting on May 12, 1727, he convinced them all to sign an agreement, "Brotherly Union and Compact," that brought a semblance of unity. This commitment was a dedication of their lives to the service of Jesus Christ in the same way he had dedicated his. In it they also renounced self-love, self-will, disobedience and freethinking, declaring that they each wished to be led by the Spirit in all things. Finally, the agreement required that they desire to love one another in "true sincerity" and to submit themselves in an accountability structure for both discipleship and prayer. The effect was almost instant. As they literally shook hands and promised to abide by the new rules, they were transformed from quarreling individuals to an organized body of believers.

Three months after this historic breakthrough in unity, which saved the community, they experienced what Zinzendorf would later call the Moravian Pentecost. On the morning of August 13, 1727, during a specially called communion service, the Spirit fell. Their hearts were set on fire for the Savior and toward each other. The sense of awe released a strong conviction of sin and an overpowering love for one another. The agreement they had signed in obedience a few weeks before suddenly became a heart commitment as the Holy Spirit Himself immersed them into one love. They felt as if the whole place had become the tabernacle of God as they finally understood that they were one in Christ. For weeks every time they met they were aware of the purifying fire of the Holy Spirit. John Greenfield, a Moravian historian, describes that day in August as a day of the outpouring of the Holy Spirit:

> We saw the hand of God and His wonders, and we were all under the cloud of our fathers baptized with their Spirit. The Holy Ghost came upon us and in those days great signs and wonders took place in our midst. From that time scarcely a day passed but what we beheld His almighty workings amongst us.... Everyone desired above everything else that the Holy Spirit might have full control. Self-love and self-will as well as all disobedience disappeared and an overwhelming flood of grace swept us all out into the great ocean of Divine Love.[7]

Herrnhut grew rapidly after this transforming Pentecost. To maintain the sense of the presence of the Holy Spirit, they set up a watch of continuous prayer 24 hours a day which ran for over 100 years. As a result of all God was doing through them, the Moravians became a major factor in Christian renewal during the 18th century. Their battle cry - "Our Lamb has conquered; let us follow Him"

They became the first large scale protestant mission organization, sending hundreds of missionaries to many parts of the world. They were the first to send out unordained "lay" people to the mission field. They were the first to go to the slaves and were the first missionaries in many countries of the world. Their passion for God became a primary influence on the Wesley brothers who would be used to birth an awakening in England.

The Moravians grasped the principle of sustained revival and maintained it for over one hundred years. We believe they were a forerunner of the kind of awakening that is at present being birthed in the earth. The harvest is ready; the need is for churches across the world to embrace a revival culture so that together we can nurture the move of the Spirit that has begun to spread. No single church or ministry is going to get the credit for what God is about to do. Don't miss this day of visitation. It is still in the infant stage and must be nurtured. How? Recognize the presence and power of God in our midst and in the church, then give ourselves to fanning the flame of revival.

In Boy Scouts we were taught to light a fire with a flint and steel. It is relatively easy to get a spark, but once the spark touches the tender it must be carefully nurtured into flame. This is how God is asking us to treat the move of His Spirit in our lives and in the church. If we will carefully steward what we are given, God will faithfully pour out more. A revival culture exists to fan the embers of revival into flame. As the flame grows we must faithfully tend the fire by adding the fuel outlined in each chapter. Throw on a log of testimony and one of hope and watch the flame of expectancy increase. Stir the embers by adding joy with a little love and watch compassion flare up in the hearts of believers.

A revival fire tended correctly will spread out of the house and into the streets as members of the body carry the fire with them wherever they go. The grocery store, the bank, and their work place are touched as they release God's goodness. Eventually, this fire will bring an awakening to our neighborhoods, our cities, our state, our nation and to the nations of the earth. Take on the challenge; it is our responsibility to nurture the awakening until the earth is filled with the glory of the Lord!

ENDNOTES

Introduction

1. Matthew Backholer, Revival Fires and Awakenings: Thirty-Six Visitations of the Holy Spirit, (ByFaith Media 2009), 29.

2. Diane Severance, Evangelical Revival in England, Salem Web Network, http://www.christianity.com/church/church-history/timeline/1701-1800/evangelical-revival-in-england-11630228.html (Dec. 2, 2013).

3. Backholer, 19.

Chapter 1 (Creating a Revival Culture)

1. Michael J. Farabee, Laws of Thermodynamics: On-Line Biology Book, Hosted by Estrella Mountain Community College, Text ©1992, 1994, 1997 - 2001, www2.estrellamountain.edu/faculty/farabee/biobk/biobookener1.html (Jan. 2, 2014).

2. www2.estrellamountain.edu/faculty/farabee/biobk/biobookener1.html

3. E.G. Carre, ed, The Life Story of John Hyde: Praying Hyde, The Apostle of Prayer, (Bridge Logos, Aachen Fl. 2004), 11.

Chapter 2 (Supernatural Lifestyle)

1. Howard Marshall, The Acts of the Apostles: An introduction and Commentary, Tyndale New Testament Commentaries, (Inter-Varsity Press, 1980), 56.

2. New Exhaustive Strong's Numbers and Concordance with Expanded Greek-Hebrew Dictionary. Copyright © 1994, 2003, 2006 Biblesoft, Inc. and International Bible Translators, Inc.).

3. Kevin Dedmon, The Ultimate Treasure Hunt: A Guide to Supernatural Evangelism through Supernatural Encounters, (Shippensburg PA, Destiny Image, 2007).

4. Bill Johnson, Hosting the Presence: Unveiling Heaven's Agenda, Publishers Inc. (Shippensburg PA, Destiny Image 2012), 88, 89.

Chapter 3 (Testimony)

1. Theological Wordbook of the Old Testament. Copyright 1980 The Moody Bible Institute of Chicago, Electronic Database by Biblesoft, Inc.

2. Ibid.

3. Edward R. Miller, Thy God Reigneth: The Story of the Argentina Revival, (Peniel Publications, 1964).

4. Brown-Driver-Briggs Hebrew Lexicon, Copyright 1993, Woodside Bible Fellowship, Ontario, Canada, Electronic Database by Biblesoft Inc.

Chapter 4 (Goodness)

1. A. W. Tozer, The Knowledge of the Holy: (STL Books, 1976), 9.

Chapter 5 (Righteousness)

1. Kittel's, Theological Dictionary of the New Testament, abridged edition, Copyright 1985 Eerdmans, Electronic Database by Biblesoft Inc.

Chapter 7 (Love)

1. New Exhaustive Strong's Numbers and Concordance.

2. Thayer's Greek Lexicon, Electronic Database. Copyright © 2000, 2003, 2006 by Biblesoft, Inc.

Chapter 8 (Honor)

1. Thayer's Greek Lexicon.

2. Vines Expository Dictionary of Biblical Words, Coptright1985, Thomas Nelson Publishers.

3. Thayer's Greek Lexicon.

Chapter 9 (Order or Life)

1. Thayers, Greek Lexicon.

2. www2.estrellamountain.edu/faculty/farabee/biobk/biobookener1.html

3. Michael J. Farabee, Laws of Thermodynamics.

Chapter 10 (Joy)

1. Robert Jamieson, A.R. Fausset and David Brown, Jameson Faucet & Brown: Commentary on the Whole Bible (John7:39).

Chapter 11 (Forgiveness)

1. Corrie Ten Boom, with John and Elizabeth Sherrill. Hiding Place: the Triumphant True Story of Corrie Ten Boom, (Chosen Books 1971), 217.

2. Ibid, 238.

3. Journal of Virtues, http://incharacter.org/archives/forgiveness/ten-great-moments-in-forgiveness-history/ (Feb. 3, 2014).

Chapter 12 (Unity)

1. Douglas Allen Foster, ed., The Encyclopedia of the Stone-Campbell Movement, (Eerdmans Publishing 2004), 688.

2. Thayer's Greek Lexicon.

3. Frank Bartleman, Another Wave Rolls In!: What Really Happened at Azusa Street(Monroeville, Pa.: Whitaker Books, 1970), 55.

4. Kittel's, Theological Dictionary of the New Testament.

5. Thayer's Greek Lexicon.

6. Joseph Edmond Hutton, A Short History of the Moravian Church: (Moravian Publication Office, 1895), 125.

7. John Greenfield, Power From On High: The story of the Great Moravian Revival of 1727, (Moravian Church, 1928), 3.